BILL BAILEY'S REMARKABLE GUIDE TO HAPPINESS

BILL BAILEY'S REMARKABLE GUIDE TO HAPPINESS

BILL BAILEY

ILLUSTRATED BY BILL BAILEY AND JOE MAGEE

Quercus

First published in Great Britain in 2020 by

Quercus Editions Ltd
Carmelite House
50 Victoria Embankment
London EC4Y 0DZ

An Hachette UK company

HB ISBN 978 1 52941 245 1
Ebook ISBN 978 1 52941 246 8

10 9 8 7 6 5 4 3 2 1
Typeset by Joe Magee
Printed and bound in Great Britain by Clays Ltd, Elcograf S.p.A.

To my family and friends, and all those
who have shared in these adventures

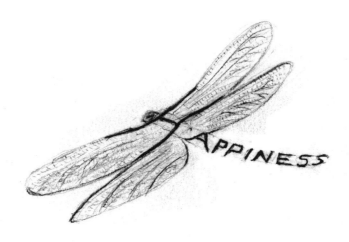

CONTENTS

FOREWORD

This book was written during the coronavirus pandemic, largely while we were in lockdown.

During this unexpected quiet time at home, I finally got around to archiving my comedy shows, and I was struck, firstly by how much longer my hair was back in the day, and secondly by how much happiness has been a subject that I have explored in my sketches and gigs over many years, to the point that it appears as a constant thread running through it all.

Happiness might seem an odd or even perverse topic to tackle during these strange times, but perhaps this whole experience has made us all take stock a little and consider what is most important, and happiness is right up there for me, along with correct footwear.

The former UN Secretary General Ban Ki-moon once said:

'Happiness is neither a frivolity nor a luxury . . . It should be denied to no one and available to all.'

I agree with the fact that it should be denied to no one, although I can't help thinking this powerful statement would work equally well if you substituted 'happiness' for 'high-speed broadband'.

I disagree, though, with the eminent Ban Ki-moon, in that I think that sometimes happiness is frivolous, and sometimes it is luxurious, and part of understanding it is knowing what kind of joy has shown up, and how to get the most from it.

In this book, I am not saying I have some secret knowledge that reveals the key to happiness. I have no magic theory, or equation, or diet.

There will be no tips on yoga, or 'harnessing the power within'.

There will be no 'ten steps to personal mastery'.

At most, there will be 'a couple of steps towards basic personal competence', that's it.

In this book, I am not telling you how to live your life. I just want to share with you a few accounts of fortuitous moments and remarkable times when I experienced something which felt to me like happiness. They might strike a chord; they might just make you smile.

CRAZY GOLF

I am standing on the first tee of a golf course, club in my hand, looking with some trepidation down the challenging narrow fairway. There are obstacles in the form of large boulders and something resembling a speed bump between me and the flag which flutters above the hole. So far so normal. But adjacent to the green, there is a terrifying-looking life-size velociraptor swaying jerkily, eyeing me with evil intent. Is this a dream? Have I been at the Costa Rican hallucinogenic plums again?

NEW YORK
1927

COME ON FRANK,
JUST HIT IT!

No, of course not, it's dinosaur mini-golf! One of the greatest and silliest inventions on the planet, and an endless source of happiness.

As the name suggests, this particular mini-golf course weaves its way around several large animatronic dinosaurs, which occasionally lurch drunkenly in your direction and roar unconvincingly. I have left many a sensible non-crazy golf course in a foul mood, cursing and vowing never to set foot on such a place ever again. I have never left a crazy golf course with anything other than a beaming smile, and this added layer of craziness makes me feel positively giddy with pleasure.

Crazy golf (or mini-golf, or miniature golf, goofy golf, adventure golf, putter golf, nutters with putters, etc.) allegedly has its origins in America, where the first commercial mini-golf course opened in Pinehurst, North Carolina, in 1916. An American golf fanatic, Thomas McCullough Fairbairn, revolutionised the game in 1922 by introducing the artificial playing surface, and suddenly mini-golf took off in a big way. By the end of the 1920s, there were tens of thousands of courses across America, including at least a hundred and fifty rooftop courses in New York City alone.

But then came the Great Depression, which brought an end to the mini-golf boom. That was it for *le golf fou*, until two enterprising Swedish brothers, Erik and Eskil Norman, who'd been living in the States and had witnessed this golfing phenomenon, brought it back to Sweden. After the Second World War, there was a burst of optimism in Europe, and with it came a desire for more leisure, and nothing says giddy escapism more than belting a rubberised golf ball through the face of a giant plastic crab. In this post-war period, crazy golf began to take root in Europe, with enthusiastic players spread across the continent, especially Germany, which saw the emergence of eleven thousand officially licensed mini-golfers. *Hürra für den Crazy Golf!*

But hold on, Bill, the origins of this tremendous sport go back a lot further.

According to the Crazy Golf Museum, evidence has been uncovered by Lanzhou University suggesting that crazy golf was first played in China. In the Dongxuan Records written during the Song Dynasty (AD960–1279) a prominent magistrate instructed his daughter to 'dig holes in the ground so that he might knock a ball into them with a specially crafted stick', which is golf in a nutshell really.

Golf was first played in St Andrews in the fifteenth century, although it was considered a man's sport. It wasn't until 1867 that women were allowed to play at the Home of Golf. Even then, they were barred from the main course, presumably lest the exertion cause them to faint into the bunkers. The fragrant wives and daughters of the male golfers were confined to a specially made, and far less strenuous, putting area, which led eventually to the creation of putting clubs around Britain, found mainly at seaside resorts. It's become an endearingly British pastime, you might say. It's all part of the diorama of the Great British Seaside Holiday: a few sunburned bonces, ice cream, fish and chips, seagulls, coastal poverty and rural dislocation. I recall many a brisk walk along a wind-whipped seafront in winter, or a hot pasty burning on my tongue, a bag of chips unwrapped on the dashboard of the car, a cozy fug steaming up the windows, my name written in the condensation. And with the British love of eccentricity I am not entirely surprised to learn that the UK has been hosting the World Crazy Golf Championships in Hastings since 2002.

And so I find myself again on the first tee of dinosaur mini-golf, lining up a putter with a pink rubber golf ball. I am here with my eight-year-old son and eighty-year-old father, which only serves to underline the inter-generational appeal of this ludicrous pastime. My dad, I have come to realise over the years, secretly loves mini-golf. He always offers to join in when I suggest a round to him, and he's always the first to the tee. This one is a straightforward hole in crazy golf terms, the only hazard being a kind of concrete speed bump halfway between tee and flag. His face becomes serious, he addresses the ball, checks the line, and strikes.

The ball runs straight down the concrete fairway, bobbles slightly, rolls over the hump, avoids the boulders, then closes in on the hole. We are all now mouths open, agog, cheering him on, and the ball continues straight into the heart of the hole and drops in. We whoop and cheer, my dad beams from ear to ear. Hole in one! Or an ace in mini-golf speak. My dad styles it out with his usual aplomb. 'That's how you do it.'

When the opportunity presents itself, seek out crazy golf, and you will not be disappointed. That moment we all shared with my dad getting a hole in one has become part of family folklore. Every time we've played since then, there's always much faux-conspiratorial muttering along the lines of, 'Watch out for Dad, he's a hustler, he's a ringer, he'll take us all to the cleaners.'

And for this I am eternally grateful to the Chinese magistrate from the Song Dynasty.

Xiè xie!

A CLEAR-OUT

2

I always think that, as mood-lifters go, having a bit of a clear-out is hard to beat.

In the name of research for this book, I found myself idly browsing the internet for some 'happiness guides'. The author of one of them had the eye-catching moniker of 'positive psychology guru', a job which was somehow overlooked by my school careers officer. I remember filling in a computerised questionnaire that was meant to process my answers and from them deduce my ideal career path. It came back with two stark options: museum curator or member of the diplomatic service. It was something of a shock, except that, as you'll see throughout this book, I have a love of antiquity, of the origin of things, and I travel around the world touring a kind of stand-up that mocks but also upholds the nature of Britishness, so I'd say this survey might have been playing the long game.

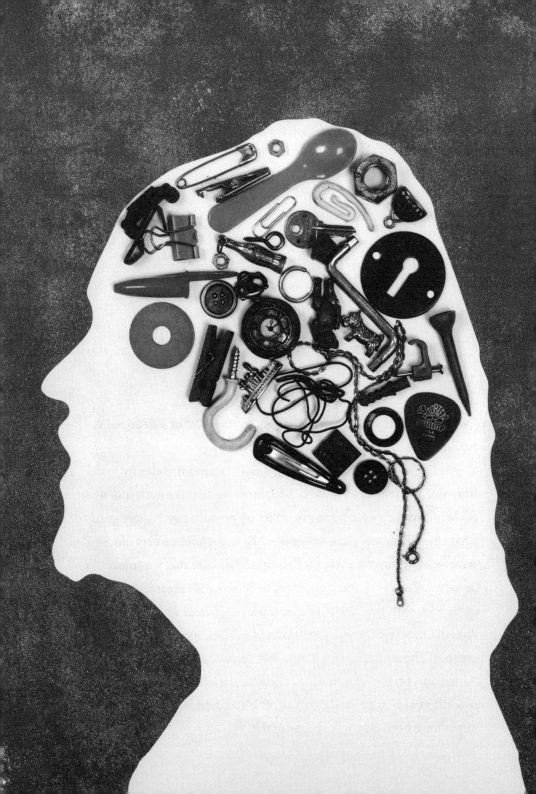

Regarding the 'positive thinking' bandwagon, I have no quibble with the fine precepts such as, 'Don't judge others, stay optimistic,' etc. But in my experience, something less high-minded and more mundane like, 'Always put the lids back on jars' will often elicit the same amount of well-being. By all means strive for a mental equilibrium by eliminating negative thinking, but while you're doing that, tidy up a bit, and chuck some stuff out. That will really help.

So here I am standing in front of my wardrobe. I'm looking at items of clothing I have inexplicably been holding on to for years. One in particular is an ill-fitting nondescript grey T-shirt that has no redeeming features. It never really felt comfortable on; it's faded and has holes around the collar. And yet I'm humming and hah-ing over it like it's a family heirloom. The flimsy reasoning for not getting rid of it is that it might come in handy for something.

Ah, but what about this lovely Chinese jacket/smock thing that I bought in a street market in Yunnan province? Yes, in rural China it seemed like a good idea. But in Hammersmith it looks ridiculous. On the very rare occasions when I've worn it in the house, I've looked like a sitcom art teacher. Or a prime-time TV drama calligraphy expert who has a secret life as an opium dealer. Either way, I will never, ever wear it in public. But then, I think, what if I'm cast in one of these roles I've just described? Better leave the jacket in the wardrobe. You never know.

When a friend came round to take me paintballing, I quizzed him on what I should wear under the protective stuff.

'Just wear an old T-shirt.'

What, like a faded one, one with holes round the collar, one that doesn't really fit?

'Yeah, that sort of thing.'

What, like this grey one?

'Perfect.'

How about this Chinese jacket over the top of it?

'No.'

Before 1994 there was no real storage industry in Britain. We had to take things to the tip or hand them down to the next generation. Removal companies offered a storage service, but we were yet to see the proliferation of huge industrial units and repurposed warehouses, which now serve as repositories for the never-used, the unworn, the unloved. You'll have seen them cropping up near you. It's a boom industry. There are now over eight hundred of them around Britain, full of stuff we can't chuck out or have no room for.

When a shiny new one opened near the M4 in west London, some faulty wiring meant the 'S' of 'Self' was not illuminated. So as you passed by, you were greeted with an enormous building that proudly declared its purpose: 'ELF STORAGE'. It was just before Christmas and it never failed to make me smile, and indeed it was a sad day when they finally fixed it.

We have become a nation of hoarders. This surely flies in the face of all the Zen simplification and eastern philosophy that we've been exposed to for decades. Still, we hang on to our unused belongings. Perhaps it's a DNA echo from our early ancestors, when storing up stuff was not just a whim, it was a survival precaution. Although I don't know what evolutionary advantage is conferred by holding on to a standard lamp and a nest of coffee tables. The self-help publishing industry only adds to the problem: there is no space for all those books on decluttering so we have to box them up and put them in storage.

Having a clear-out often encourages you to confront your former self, and I welcome the clarity of thought that makes you put your things in the 'keep' or 'chuck' pile. And it's not just about the extra space. There is a slight smug feeling of being wiser. Looking at all this nonsense and shaking your head, asking yourself, 'What was I thinking?', is a great way of putting some distance between the current you and the younger, more impulsive you.

Recently, I dug out some items I'd brought back from a Glastonbury Festival years ago: an ornamental mobile made out of bent spoons; a metal chicken made from old engine parts; a jester's hat. To assess their fate, I lay them out on the garden table, like exhibits in a trial.

You can agonise over some item or other for ages, but when you finally get around to slinging it out, you hardly think of it again. I've realised that it's not really the love for the object itself that causes me to hesitate, but rather an unwillingness on my part to make the decision. We cling on, deferring the moment of casting out, to avoid dissonance, perhaps even to avoid disappointment. Most of the time we resist change because it seems too much of a wrench, or it's just too much hassle, and letting go of something you may have hefted around from place to place is undoubtedly tough.

From now on, when it comes to choosing precious objects that are freighted with memory that I really can't let go of, I try to pick small, handy stuff I can get into a shoebox, roll up in a cardboard tube, or even better, fit in a plastic takeaway carton with a sealable lid.

Keep the storage space down.

This will lead to Happy Days.

The spoon mobile and the metal chicken went to the charity shop.

I kept the jester's hat, though.

Might come in handy.

WILD SWIMMING

3

I'm in Iceland with my now teenage son a short drive from Reykjavik, at Silfra Creek, on the shores of Lake Thingvellir, where we are about to immerse ourselves in the icy meltwater from the Langjökull Glacier. Shivering in the car park, stripped of our outer layers, we grapple with cumbersome drysuits, the ice-covered material uncooperative under our numbed fingers. Unlike wetsuits which are protective but permeable, drysuits keep you dry by forming a watertight seal around your neck and wrists, allowing you to wear clothes underneath. I make full use of this feature with my two pairs of socks, thermals, jeans and two T-shirts. The previous group of ice-creek swimmers have recently divested themselves of these damp neoprene husks, which, chilled by the biting wind, have now frozen stiff. They stand of their own accord, propped up against a fence, looking like the sloughed-off skin of a man-walrus, a manrus if you will, or a White Walker's onesie. Just to unthaw my suit I have to pour boiling water over it.

Needless to say, I am still very apprehensive. I might get cold shock, have an asthma attack, then what? My son looks nervous; we all look nervous. Even our implausibly cheery Icelandic guide doesn't appear entirely comfortable. What the hell are we doing?

The water looks calm, protected as it is by a deep gully from a scouring wind, which whips round my ears and chills this already cold October day down to minus ten degrees Celsius. The water temperature, we have been told by our guide, is going to be around two degrees. So positively balmy then. In the distance, blocks of ice bob ominously around the shoreline. This ancient fissure is a wild place, and stunning with it, but the harsh beauty of its crystal-clear water doesn't at this stage justify the fact that it's a freezing river in which we are about to become immersed.

My son checks the settings on the GoPro camera, and fixes me

18

with a disbelieving glare before muttering into his snorkel, 'Whose idea was this again?'

Iceland is a place of stark and surreal magnificence, of vast lava fields, hot springs, waterfalls and huge open valleys, and the largest consumption of Pepsi Max in Europe (actually, I can't vouch for this, but I did witness huge buckets of the stuff being slurped down in a multiplex cinema in Reykjavik). Icelanders love going to the movies, and judging by the bitter cold I was now experiencing outdoors, I can understand why. But despite the austere nature of the latitude and the almost complete absence of trees, Icelanders, all 350,000 of them, are among the happiest people on Earth.

They have many reasons to be fearful for the future of their country. Their glaciers, the largest in Europe, could melt within a century, which on a planetary timescale might be classed as imminent. I know this because I've met landscapes under climate strife that are disappearing at a markedly slower rate. Once I drove out to the Bungle Bungle rock formations in the Kimberley Ranges of North Western Australia. The Bungle Bungles are deep valleys of smooth bluish rock, weathered with such strange regularity that they resemble a vast art installation. My guide told me solemnly that they were 350 million years old, but because of climate change, and man-made depredations to our planet, there's a good chance they won't be here in 150 million years.

'Got here just in time then,' I quipped, but my guide's expression was as blank as the rocks themselves.

Standing among these ancient behemoths, and taking in their silent, implacable antiquity, my size and significance began to shrink as I was struck by the gadfly nature of the human lifespan. We are born, we flit about, we find a mate, we try to make sense of it all, then we're gone – pfffffft – during which time the Bungle Bungles did nothing, except perhaps grow a layer of lichen.

I swam in the Firth of Forth on a whim one year when I was performing at the Edinburgh Festival. We took a picnic to Gullane Beach, just outside the city. It was a sunny day, almost warm in fact, and the tepid sunlight must have made us giddy with excitement. Goaded by encouraging voices, I was dared to take a dip. It was an act of haggis-fuelled bravado, bordering on recklessness. I had no swimwear but my natural shyness, combined with a deal of concern

for the eyes of others, prevented skinny dipping. Although I might
just as well have been naked for all the protection my thin boxer
shorts afforded against the icy embrace of the North Sea.

I had never known such cold before that moment, and I think
my body took a while to register, as if in disbelief. My entire sensory
system was momentarily cauterised by the searing chill, but as nerve
endings began sputtering back to life, my whole body started to

tingle, quiver with pain, then scream NOOOO!

Despite the trauma of that day I have since become a keen wild swimmer. Every time I have emerged from some body of open water, I have felt more alive, energised, and a bit feral. But right now, staring down this iceberg-laden creek, I'm doubting my nerve to take the plunge.

As we step off the stairwell into the water, I brace myself for the extreme cold – which thankfully I don't feel. The suit and the thermal clothing see to that. What is a shock is when the water comes into contact with the tiny patch of exposed skin on my temples, the bit that is not covered by my suit or my mask. Also, the mittens don't quite cut it keeping the hands warm.

I gradually get accustomed to the restrictive drysuit, but progress is slow and ungainly. My movement in the water, normally so graceful and otter-like, becomes slow and comically inept. I float away from the metal stairs clutching my camera by its hand-grip and try to turn to capture the view looking back down the creek, but succeed only in rolling onto my back and flailing ineffectually with my arms, like a drunk dugong.

The water, while just above freezing, is amazingly clear, gin-clear. A thought flits into my head about the etiquette of snorkelling in a gin creek, and whether you could add tonic. The sunlight filters down and turns the deeper water into a palette of stunning blues, from cerulean to cobalt to the delicate turquoise of a shallow Orcadian bay. The underwater view is one of a deep fissure covered in a vast jumble of volcanic rock deposited there over many lifetimes. It is spectacular and eerily beautiful, and the icy water pressing round my temples intensifies the whole experience.

After what seems like a few minutes of paddling, my hands start to feel a little numb, but otherwise I am OK, and I say to myself in an American accent, 'I got this!' but I have a snorkel in my mouth so it comes out more like, 'I yot yis,' like a bad ventriloquist with his motivational puppet.

Suddenly, I am told to get out. *Aha*, I think, *something's happened, someone's bailed. Phew! Glad it wasn't me, I'm fine, lovin' it. Too cold for you, wusses?* The plan was to be in the water for thirty-five minutes. Which was, as it turned out, the exact amount of time I was in the water. I had to check the GoPro footage before I believed it. Something happened to me in the creek, time just fast-forwarded, like Jodie Foster's alien encounter in the film *Contact*. We go straight to a café and eat soup in stunned silence.

That was an extreme wild swim, no doubt about it. I still, even now, can't quite believe we had the bottle to do it. I might not be leaping into

Fig. 1 - *Bilrus*

another glacial fissure anytime soon, but I'm glad we had a dip in this one. It was worth it for the dreamlike images captured on my camera and the slight air of peril that permeated the whole endeavour.

But there's something else of value here. It was deeply satisfying to take a trip outside my comfort zone, to test my mettle in this way. It felt like I'd banked a little self-reliance that I might later draw on in times of strife. It was certainly revitalising, thrilling even. The post-swim high lasted for many weeks.

Iceland has plenty of places and experiences like this: we walked over lava fields, descended into extinct volcanos and chased the Northern Lights around the outskirts of Reykjavik with adrenaline-fuelled Aurora hunters. This is a place where physical challenges go hand in hand with a greater appreciation of nature, and a sense of personal achievement, something which you'll see is dear to my heart.

Iceland regularly features in the top five of happy countries, yet according to the *Nordic Labour Journal*, income accounts for 1 per cent of the reason for Icelanders' happiness. I can see what the remaining 99 per cent is made up of: they have other paths to happiness, other routes to a richer life, by feeling connected to their surroundings, to belonging, to discovering a deep-rooted sense of identity. But to really thrive here, in this unforgiving place, you need resilience to endure life's challenges, a toughness borne out of glacial proximity. Hardship is not just something you might overcome to be happy, it's a necessity, a yardstick by which to measure the good times. According to Dóra Guðmundsdóttir, governmental psychologist at Iceland's Directorate of Health, happiness is what's left after you've been through joy and sorrow. It's something worn, weathered, enduring.

A bit Bungle Bungle-y.

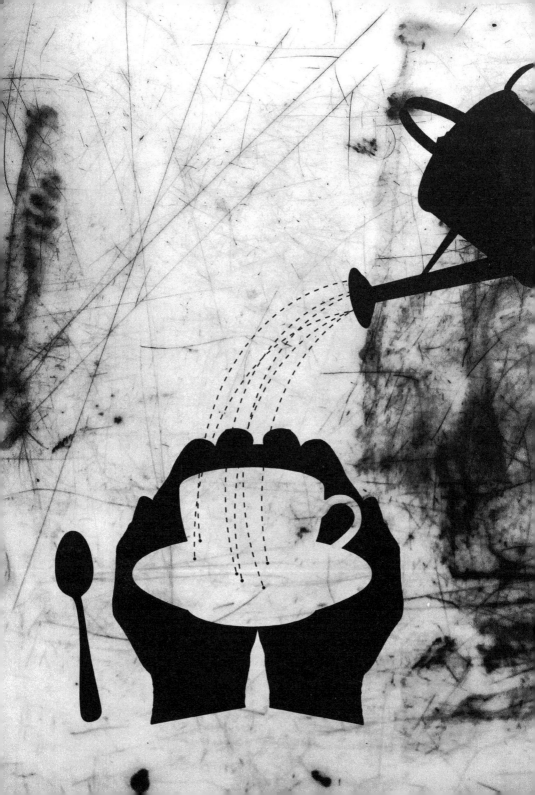

LITTLE THINGS

4

Every morning, I have a routine. I use a small hand-press coffee making kit to make coffee for me and my wife. It's become a daily ritual, a little coffee-based ceremony that is a physical action, an act of nurture, a mindful thing, a meditative moment. So many boxes are ticked.

What I really love about this machine is its simplicity. I am a huge lover of gadgets, of tech generally, and the more sophisticated, the better. But this I make an exception for. There's no power cable, no setting up, no fancy settings to blunder through without checking a manual.

It's also generous in its allowance for human error as the press has a large base, a practical design feature to allow it to fit over most mugs, so even a ham-fisted disorderly gibbon such as myself can operate it. Over time, I have perfected the art, using just the right amount of coffee, refining the stirring time, the dispensing of grounds, the cleansing, the storage. I know how to live.

I take this with me everywhere. In fact, I bought it while on a stand-up tour, so I could make a decent cup of coffee in hotels around the world. The whole kit fits into its own zip-up bag, and to avoid disappointment I always pack some ground coffee, which I have found travels best stuffed into a shoe, and held in place with a hiking sock before being packed artfully in my suitcase. I say this only because so

27

many hotels seem to have been love-bombed by the George Clooney marketing people, and each one now proudly displays a Nespresso machine. There are some who swear by them. Personally, I can't abide these pod-gorging charlatans, these false prophets of coffee deliverance. My humble hand-press is far superior, so good that I have two of them, a home one, and a touring one – yes, readers, I know, I am a creature of excess.

Regardless of my mood, of the weather, or whatever crisis is gripping the world at that moment, coffee time is a fixed point around which the rest of the day flows. On tour, often the days begin to blur together, so a small daily act like making coffee takes on a greater significance. I find it reassuring and comforting. It brings me a small, Morris-Minor-Traveller-glove-box-light glow of contentment.

Sometimes, you can string a few of these victories together for a hat-trick of happiness. The day I made two perfect cups of coffee, baked some low-sugar brownies and assembled a simple yet stylish table will live long in the memory. If I'd also managed to tidy my studio, mow the lawn and fix the dishwasher, I'd have probably taken the rest of the week off.

The dishwasher, when I finally got around to repairing it, was a particular challenge, only because of an unforeseen problem. I had a glance at the manual, but quickly thought to myself, *Too many words, blah blah blah . . . I don't need this, I will be resourceful. I will do what every sensible person does, I will look it up on YouTube.* What the otherwise helpful vid didn't say was how dark it is inside a dishwasher. The demo one on the video seemed to be lit up like a cruise ship on New Year's Eve.

I groped around tentatively in the grey, soapy water that had collected over the drain in the near dark, cursing and grunting with the effort of holding my ungainly frame in a 'maintenance crouch'. Using the skills of modern man, I expertly activated my phone's torch function and wedged it into the mug and glass upper shelf, shedding perfect light onto the drain. Result!

However, not so ingeniously, I now couldn't see the relevant YouTube video. After what seemed like a new epoch in man's evolution, and much memorising of the video's key instructions, before wedging my phone back in the ramekin level, I found the culprit. Victory! My years of piano playing paid off, as my Chopin-toughened fingers removed the obstruction of a piece of broken wine glass, which I dropped, hospital drama-like, into a stainless-steel bowl. Once I'd finally manipulated the wayward plastic valve back into place, I cried, 'Yes!' A man shouting from within a domestic appliance is an unusual sight and it attracted the attention of our four dogs, who gathered in a semi-circle near the dishwasher, much like a crowd would with a street-performer.

'OK, everyone,' I said. 'Show's over.'

The dogs didn't move. They clearly knew something I didn't. There was more entertainment to come.

As I tried to lever myself out, I banged my head on the underside, swore, stubbed my toe getting up, swore again, lost my balance, put my hand down on the plastic rack and bent one of its tines.

The dogs wagged their tails in silent applause.

MUSIC

5

One of my earliest memories is of hearing my mother singing around
the house. She would often accompany songs on the radio. Perry
Como's 'Magic Moments' was a favourite. It's a classic of its genre. How
many songs can you say have a whistled refrain and a jaunty bassoon
counterpoint? Not many, and certainly not one by the band Slipknot,
although Slipknot do feature in another of my vivid musical memories.
Standing stageside at Sonisphere Festival in 2011, I watched them whip
a rain-soaked crowd into a frenzy. This sonic assault is the music I
imagine orcs listen to before going into battle.

Visualising music is a habit I acquired in childhood. From an
early age my mother would sit me down near the record player and
bring music to life. A favourite of mine I now know was the *Karelia
Suite* by Sibelius, but back then I had no idea who the composer
was, or what the piece was called. I had no expectation, or frame
of reference. For that reason, I think of it now as one of the purest
forms of musical enjoyment I can recall. My mother would describe
the scenes that the music seemed to suggest to her. Over the opening
bars of distant horns and rising layers of rhythmic, building strings,
she would say, 'These are horsemen riding through a forest, over a
mountain, their flags waving.' Even now, whenever I hear this music,
I see an army on horseback at dawn, resplendent in full battledress,
standards fluttering a little in the breeze, the horses trotting through

31

the mist as the sun's rays begin to burst over the mountains.

This is noble, irresistible music like the powerful Nordic opening to Sibelius's *Finlandia*. Now that I've been to Finland, though, the stark, diminished fifth chords and the brooding darkness of the music is strangely disconnected from the Finland I've seen. This discordant clash of brass and whirling strings seems to be describing Mordor, not the tranquil beauty of pine forests and of a thousand glittering lakes, where doughty Finns relax by their lakeside cabins, their hearts aglow with social cohesion. To me, this music conjures up a fleet of Imperial Star Destroyers gliding malevolently over a rebel stronghold, or a twelve-foot model of an ant being slowly wheeled out of a lock-up garage.

Music is in many ways an enigmatic human activity. It exists in virtually every culture across the world, yet only a few early instruments survive. There are no written accounts to explain how *Homo sapiens* first discovered the love of a good tune. Perhaps when our ancestors heard lilting birdsong, wind in the trees or the pounding hooves of fleeing deer, it provoked in them an emotional response. After the hunting was done, they would reflect, and try to recreate these sounds that caused pleasurable sensations in their developing brains. This might explain the Palaeolithic bone flutes found in southern Germany that were made around forty thousand years ago. A crudely hewn vulture's wing bone with five holes was the first step on a path that led eventually to Mozart's Flute Concerto No. 1 in G major.

The world of science puzzles over music, and whether it conferred an evolutionary advantage on our ancestors. I think on balance that it did. Those early melodies worked their magic on our bearded forebears, making them gaze rheumily into a fire, but it had a practical application too. The rituals of music helped to codify shared myths and promote greater social bonds. Although for a few individuals it actually might have been a disadvantage. I picture one of my Neanderthal relatives dragging a wild boar back to his cave, and something causing him to dally. Ah, the silvery song of a goldfinch! He pauses, his whiskery face twitching into a smile. A stirring of wistfulness in his oversize yet clumsy frame compels him to let his guard down, and he is immediately spatchcocked by a giant ground sloth.

Whatever its origins, music is inextricably linked with human emotions. When I hear music that affects me (like for instance Rachmaninoff's Piano Concerto No. 2) I think, whoever's written this must also have felt longing or regret, anger, giddy lightness, been bored or crazy in love or just exasperated by life in general. And for me, knowing this is reassuring. If someone else has felt these same emotions that correspond to mine, then somehow the world is briefly not such a bewildering place.

We're not alone in our thoughts, and these same feelings have echoed down the ages.

For me, music is a companion, a source of happiness and sometimes comfort, and my curiosity at its power over us has been my mother's gift to me.

Fig. 2 - *What I sometimes visualise
when national anthems play*

CARING FOR PLANTS

6

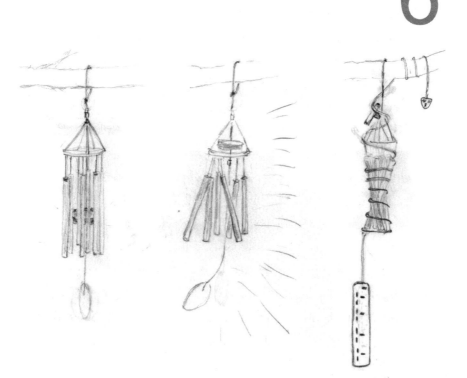

It's a cold blustery night in London as I write this. The windchimes hanging on the laurel tree in the back garden are clanging violently and out of sync, like open spot night at the bellringing club. Worried the noise will disturb the neighbours, I venture out to muffle them. There's an ingenious device on the central cord that holds the round clapper. It's a small adjustable toggle, rather like the one on the hood of your waterproof jacket. If you pinch it, it slides upwards, pushing the clanger with it above the height of the chimes, in the no-clang zone.

That's the theory anyway, but tonight the wind surges round the laurel tree with such devilish ferocity, the clapper is redundant anyway; the chimes are ding-donging together with the evil dissonance of Satan's doorbell. Ingenious design be damned then, so I resort to Bloke Solutions™ and, grabbing the central cord, I wind it around the chimes and tie it off in a rough granny knot. It's not pretty, but it seems to work.

While I'm there, I check on my tiny floral charge. It's become a nightly ritual, this garden obeisance. A few weeks previously I was staying at a hotel in Devon while I performed at venues in the area. I was there for a week, and as a parting gift the hotel presented me with a small strawberry plant in a tiny earthenware pot. I nearly left it for the next guest, but it looked so forlorn on my little table, pleading with me with huge Pikachu eyes in plant form, and something about its cheerful greenery appealed to me, so I took it with me.

Back home, it got loaded in with some touring gear, and sat on a flight case for a bit, looking out of sorts. It reminded me suddenly of Slash, the hat-wearing Guns N' Roses guitarist. I once saw an interview with him where he talked about being dropped off at his house after a tour, and about standing outside it thinking, *Now what?* I found myself checking the plant more regularly, making sure it was fed and watered, and it carried on sitting there on the flight case.

I went online to look at tips for strawberry plant care. Apparently coffee grounds are good for nurturing it. So every morning, my ritual of making coffee took on an added dimension. I began saving the coffee grounds in a plastic tub, then carefully bedding some around the stem with a teaspoon, and as the days became warmer, I moved the plant to its new home in the garden. Once out of the house and out of sight, I couldn't quite believe that I was starting to fret about this plant, wondering what it was up to, worrying that it had enough light and water. I am not a constant gardener, but this *Fragaria x ananassa* was getting to me.

One night in March after days of warmth, the barometer fell, and the air grew chilly, the sky winterish. That next morning, I was up early, barefoot and shivering in shorts and a thin T-shirt out in the garden, checking on the plant. The sky was a chalk-hill blue, marred only by a few scurrying clouds, herded north by a sheepdog wind. They seemed to be headed in the direction of Wormwood Scrubs Prison, as if late for visiting hours. What am I saying . . . Clouds visiting their relatives in Cloud Prison? I may have been left with my thoughts too long.

The little strawberry newcomer was now sharing a border with some larger pals, so I prised back their leaves and tilted the pot towards the bright sunlight. And there it was, a pale, off-white flower with a yellow centre. I felt a burst of pride. I held it aloft like Simba in

The Lion King. I quietly sang 'The Circle of Life' under my breath but then realised this would imply I'd been reincarnated as a plant. Which, as long as I worked my way fairly rapidly through the plant kingdom to eagle, I'd be happy with.

Just being around greenery can be enough to lift our spirits. We have this evolutionary tendency to favour the natural environment over the man-made, and this love of nature, this 'biophilia', is present in us all. It's no surprise to me that studies show plants, and the care of plants that involves getting your hands into the soil, can lower blood pressure and increase focus and alertness. An article published in *Science World* reveals that a mycobacterium found in soil can improve brain function, because it increases the production of serotonin in the brain, one of the 'happy' chemicals.

What I got from this plant is all this and more. It is aesthetically pleasing, beautiful even. The bright green furl of new leaves pushes up from the soil in a tightly rolled elliptical tower, a miniature Gherkin on a Lilliput skyline. Tending to something, watching it grow and flourish in a strange and surreal time, took on a disproportionate importance. If I were to go in for analysing myself in a cod-psychological way, I might say I was projecting my own fears about looking after my family and that I felt a greater responsibility to feed them, keep them safe, and this plant had become a symbol of that. But as I say, I don't go in for that.

Two months later, on a warm day in May, the first tiny green strawberries have appeared. I sit on the back step and feel an almost parental sense of pride that my care and nurturing is helping this little plant to grow and thrive.

Oh, sweet child of mine.

Fig. 3 - *Visiting Time at Cloud Prison*

RESTRAINT

7

The slogan 'Just Say No' was part of the Reagan administration campaign's 'War on Drugs' in the 1980s and 90s. It's a powerful phrase, but just saying 'No' only works if the question immediately preceding it is, 'Do you want some drugs?' Confronted with any form of nuance in the question, and the mere statement of 'No' starts to unravel. For example, if you found yourself in the Amazon jungle, staying with local tribes, and, out of politeness to his guest, a Yanomami tribesman said to you, 'Do you mind if I blow this powdered hallucinogenic bark up your nostril?' 'No . . . wait, hold on . . .' you can see how the phrase might be problematic.

That aside, 'Just Say No' is not a bad mantra by which to achieve a degree of happiness. It's handy when you're offered cakes, biscuits and other temptations. Another profiterole? No, thanks. Caramel wafer? No. Oh, go on then. Sometimes it's hard to say no to yourself. Another episode of the latest Netflix futuristic drama, a dystopian vision of a planet powered entirely by sarcasm? Sounds great.

Restraint, like so many small acts of will, is tough but immensely rewarding. Particularly when saying no is not an option, as I found out when I went to Los Angeles Zoo.

The warning signs were there. Near the entrance to the zoo, I noticed quite a few cafés and fast food joints either side of the wide pathway. Waffle houses, burger joints, hot dog and taco stands, steak restaurants, fried chicken shops, muffin kiosks, bagel stalls and ice cream parlours formed a gaudy boulevard of battered dreams. I think I counted twenty or so high-carb opportunities before we saw so much as a meerkat. In fact, I'd begun to think there was no zoo, that this was some artful installation where we were the zoo, and other snarky individuals were observing us on TV monitors. 'Look at them,' they'd be snickering. 'Look at those slack-jawed drooling goofballs...

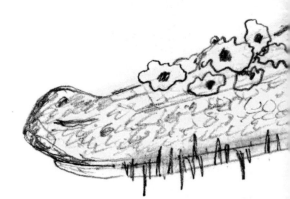

Let's see how many burritos they scarf down before they realise it's not actually a zoo.'

Our first non-snack encounter was not, actually, a meerkat but a male peacock, who seemed perky enough, but then peacocks always look reasonably chipper. However, the chimps, of which there were about a half dozen, seemed listless and bored, like seagulls loafing on a beach in winter. Not surprising, I thought. When there are more café's than chimps, there is something awry in the philosophy of this place.

The crowds were excitable and ill-disciplined. A party of schoolkids threw some popcorn over the wall at a spectacled caiman, and a few others followed suit until the teacher told them off sharply. I looked down at the croc. He had a dusting of popcorn on top of his snout, and bore an expression of withering contempt. I imagined him thinking, *That's it . . . lean out a little further, drop the popcorn, keep leaning out . . .*

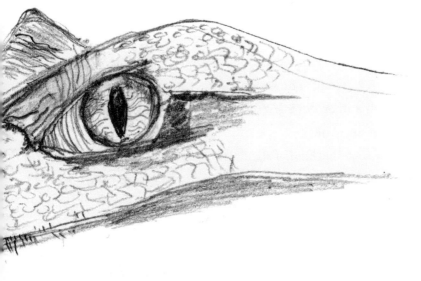

We queued for some lunch at a little shack. We chose a sandwich each, coffee and some bottles of water. This modest purchase somehow entitled me to a free supersize upgrade. The baseball-capped youth working the till with a name badge stating 'Corey' handed me an enormous bag of crisps. I mean, it was a huge bag, the like of which is not available to us in the UK. It was the size of a bag of barbecue charcoal, or a sack of logs from the garage. If you tipped this whole bag of crisps out, you could reasonably serve them in a wheelbarrow. I declined them. 'No thanks.'

Corey, clearly thinking I hadn't understood, said, 'They're free, sir.'

'Yes, I am aware of that, and it's a kind offer, but we're fine, thank you.'

A look of blank incomprehension was frozen on Corey's face. For a moment, I thought he had grasped the notion.

'But they're free, sir.'

'I know they are free, I understand the concept of free stuff, but we're quite happy with these huge sandwiches.'

Long pause.

'But they're free.'

I started another polite rebuttal, along the lines of 'I know it's hard to understand that I would turn down free stuff . . .' but I never got any further, because at that moment a grizzled old timer behind me in the queue grunted, 'Just take 'em!'

He'd obviously seen this kind of standoff before: polite Brit meets unstoppable force of American largesse. It was only going to end one way, and the quicker I accepted the inevitable, the better. Plus, the queue behind me was getting tetchy.

So, I took the village-sized bag of crisps and gave them to an incredulous couple from Idaho, Norm and Patty Prebble, who seemed overwhelmed by my act of generosity.

Patty in particular was beside herself. 'We couldn't possibly, sir!'

'It's fine, my father eats very little, and as you can see, the packet is as big as my son, so we can't possibly eat them.'

'Are you sure? It seems awfully generous.'

'Yes, I'm sure, it would be my pleasure.'

'Well, let me give you something.'

'JUST TAKE 'EM!'

We live in a time of the most conspicuous consumption in human history, and as a consequence of that it is the hardest perhaps it's ever been to say no. We are constantly assailed by entreaties to buy, to watch, even to find love. It feels as though more than ever we are encouraged to say yes more often, to consume, get involved, otherwise we'd be missing out. In 2013 the *Oxford English Dictionary* added the word FOMO, an acronym of 'Fear of Missing Out'. This word had become ubiquitous, as it sold the shiny idea that there was this exciting, spangly world out there that you just had to be a part of, and somehow everyone else knew about it, and was living *la vida loca*. Driven by social media, this insidious four-letter meme eventually became a source of unhappiness, as we now all know from reading the health pages of various magazines and newspapers.

If restraint has taught me anything, it's that saying no occasionally is not that hard, and is a good habit to acquire. It's a small act of self-care that might take you down a path to happiness, and even bring about a little LOSI (Love of Staying In).

SINGING

8

Singing is one of our most ancient urges, one that connects us to our tribal past and fills us with happiness. It is one of the oldest forms of human art, which we have appropriated from the natural world.

I can imagine that when our ancestors heard a song thrush, they would feel compelled to sit momentarily and gaze wistfully across a lake. The melodious carolling of the goldfinch stirred the soul of even the most knotty-browed Neanderthal. Even the sighing of the wind in the trees maybe inspired a Neolithic Ronan Keating to look deeply into the night and sing about life being a rollercoaster, despite not knowing what a rollercoaster was at that point.

When we sing, our whole body is the instrument. It thrums and shakes, our ribcage vibrates, our airway hums and a light goes on behind our eyes. We become more mentally alert. Singing develops the lungs, as we breathe more deeply and draw more oxygen into the

blood, causing better circulation. Our immune system is boosted. We stand up straighter, we have better posture. It also releases stored muscle tension and decreases the levels of the stress hormone cortisol in the blood. We experience an endorphin rush, which makes us feel good. It boosts the endocrine system. So you can sing a mournful Leonard Cohen song, and it will still make you happy! Hallelujah!

Singing in public is at best seen as the preserve of the busker, at worst that of the intoxicated, the annoying, the downright doolally. This is one of the reasons why churches are so important.

I am not especially religious but of all the gatherings of that nature I've attended, there is one part in which I engage fully: the singing. To stand in a church and sing hymns with others is one of life's great pleasures. I belt them out joyfully, trying to harmonise where possible, my voice wavering only as I follow an unfamiliar tune.

A spot of choral singing not only helps you live longer, it's also useful for socially awkward situations.

One time, as part of an international contingent of performers at a comedy festival in New Zealand, I was given the traditional Māori greeting of the 'hongi', the charming ritual of touching noses and foreheads.

It's not often that you are this close to a stranger. This curious and intimate act proves awkward for some of us uptight Brits, who struggle to maintain eye contact at the best of times. Undeterred, I leaned in to a benevolent elder, our foreheads and then the bridges of our noses touching. I realised I'd never done this to anyone, not even my wife. Our heads now bent towards each other, the elder looked deeply into my eyes. Because I am British, I tried to avoid eye contact, which is tricky when our eyes were almost touching. My eyes flicked left and right, up and down, rolling around in my sockets like marbles, making me look like I was having a seizure or about to start speaking in tongues.

After embarrassing myself with my eye dance, more humiliation was to come. My fellow performers and I were treated to a beautiful Māori song of greeting. We applauded, but when we stopped they looked at us expectantly as we all stood about awkwardly, until someone told us that is was customary to sing a song back.

We were a disparate bunch, a motley crew of comedians and performers from round the world. My mind raced to find a song that we would all know. A scene flashed into my brain, as often happens in these moments. It was from the film *One from the Heart*, a lost masterpiece by Francis Ford Coppola from 1982, where Frederic Forrest's character Hank is trying to stop his girlfriend Frannie, played by Teri Garr, from leaving the country to go to Bora Bora. He makes a last-ditch appeal as she boards the aircraft by singing 'You Are My Sunshine'. He's goofy and awkward and not the greatest singer, but there is something so sweet and heartfelt about it.

I snapped back into the moment and, facing our expectant Māori, I found myself singing the first line of the song. And then the whole comedy gang joined in. It was to this day one of the most surreal and wonderful moments I can recall. Yes, it was goofy and awkward, and we weren't the greatest singers, but there was something sweet and heartfelt about it. And maybe we added a few weeks to our lifetimes, who knows.

SPORT

9

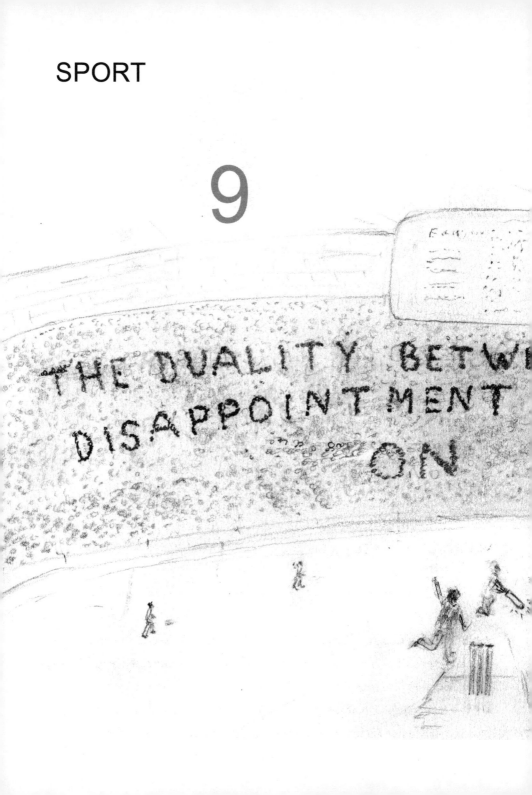

N HAPPINESS AND
S NOT LOST
US

One of the obstacles to achieving happiness, particularly in Britain, is disappointment. I know this because of my involvement in the world of entertainment. Theatre shows, musicals, concerts and indeed comedy gigs are often advertised with the same nagging invocation: 'Book early to avoid disappointment!' But what happens if you book early, yet still find yourself disappointed? Is this not the essence of life's unfairness? The beating heart of the human condition?

'I prepared, I planned, I trusted to fortune, yet I was betrayed. Like Arcite in Chaucer's "The Knight's Tale", I have prepared for the joust, I have trained to win the hand of the fair Emily and avoid disappointment, but in the end, after all that, by a random act of chance, it was my rival Palamon who has won the heart of King Theseus's daughter, Emily.'

'Sorry, sir, I'm confused. Have you made a booking or not?'

'Yes, yes, but what is the good of that, when so much of life is futile?'

Are we so risk averse, so wary of being downcast, that disappointment should be avoided? After all, it's the flip side of happiness, and when it flips back, the feelings of joy and relief are intensified. Disappointment gives us a good dose of yin that makes the yang of happiness even yangier. Better to just try and embrace it, I always find. These are the first words of my stand-up show, by way of introduction: 'I'm English, and I crave disappointment.' If you're prepared for it, if you accept it as one of life's constants, then it's not such a blow when it shows up, as it inevitably will.

I've often said, UK Happiness™ is quite different from its other global counterparts. Most people of the world, when asked about a good experience, like a holiday, will say, 'It was fantastic, we booked early, the food was great, the weather was amazing, the rooms were very clean, you could eat your dinner off the trouser press, not that we did, haha.' (N.B. I once tried to heat up a club sandwich in a hotel trouser press with no success. In an entirely unrelated incident, I once toasted a falafel on a travel iron.)

British holidaymakers are less fulsome in their trip assessment. Because we have been conditioned to expect disappointment, we are cautiously downbeat about things we have actually enjoyed. 'How was the Lake District?' 'Could have been a lot worse.' 'Niagara Falls?' 'Not too bad.' 'Great Wall of China?' 'It was all right. I mean, at the end of the day it's just a wall.' 'Hotel?' 'OK, but the tea and coffee-making facilities left a lot to be desired, and there were crumbs on the iron.'

If you're actively looking for disappointment, look no further than the world of sport.

If you follow a team, a club or a country, you will have felt its sting. There are not many more potent figures in our culture than the sporting hero. Their failures remind us that we are all human, and they are prone to the same weakness and frailty that we feel. And their successes remind us of what we are capable of, with a lot of practice, talent and a degree of luck.

And so it was, in the late summer of 2019, that I was driving through rural Sweden with some friends and family. The countryside that rolled past was about as typically Swedish as you could get. Superbly maintained roads wound through green pasture and social equality. We barrelled along past endless identical red-painted wooden houses, all similarly well maintained and nicely positioned at pleasingly regular intervals as they adorned the glittering lakes and pine forest with orderly sensible Swedishness.

Outside the car, it was textbook Scandi. Inside the car, it was quintessential Englishness. We were drinking tea, listening to the cricket commentary on the radio – in this case, the Ashes. I've loved cricket since I was a kid and when my grandad first purchased a colour television, I would sit for hours with him watching the Test match coverage. Long minutes would amble by where nothing much happened other than the soft murmuring of the crowd. This ambient hum was for me the summer sound of my childhood.

As another Swedishly wooden cabin hove into view, inside the car high drama was unfolding. It was the third Test at Headingley, and England were in trouble, and most likely going to be bowled out and lose the match, and with it the Ashes. Australia were already 1–0 up

in the series after a win and a draw, so with only two to play, a lead of 2–0 would be unassailable. But at 1–1, the Ashes would be kept alive, and who knew what might happen. Could ace batsman Ben Stokes somehow hold on? Could he get the runs?

The tension in the car was unbearable. Wickets tumbled! A near run-out! Some tea spilled into the cup holder! Another lovely red house trundled past, but we were oblivious to it. As anyone who's followed English cricket will know, disappointment is a constant companion, a weasel dæmon to our human happiness. We were braced for it, but we were equally riveted by hope.

Then, the seemingly impossible happened. Ben Stokes crashed the winning four runs through the covers, and we were ecstatic! Chaotic scenes in the vehicle ensued when I punched the roof of the hire car with delight, hit the sun visor and dislodged the rental agreement. We knew, deep down, that this was a temporary feeling, that England would probably lose the Ashes, and normal disappointment would be resumed, but that wasn't going to spoil the moment.

This is where disappointment is the great boon companion to its opposite number, happiness.

When a rare moment of brilliance, luck, or a combination of both happens in a sporting occasion in which you are totally invested, you find yourself weightless with exhilaration.

We pulled into an immaculately maintained service station, leapt from the vehicle and danced a jig of pure joy in a tidy Swedish car park. Some Swedish police watched us quizzically from their Volvo, perhaps deciding whether to offer us some leaflets about local jig-dancing courses. In Britain we would have been breathalysed.

But for a moment, we danced away the heartache, danced away the blues.

ART

10

I am in the Stedelijk Museum in Amsterdam, walking around an exhibition entitled *Chagall, Picasso, Mondrian and Others: Migrants in Paris.*

There's Modernism on show here, Cubism, Fauvism . . . all the greats. There's something about the playfulness of this lot, the cartoonish exaggerations, the fantastical and darkly surreal that appeals to me hugely. There's plenty of brilliant artwork on display here, but to me, something of the richness of colour means I am drawn continually to Chagall. The saturation – the sheer amount of it – seems like it would overwhelm a painting, but Chagall's great skill of course transforms it into something extraordinary and captivating. Picasso said of Chagall in the 1950s, 'When Matisse dies, Chagall will be the only painter left who understands what colour really is.'

The exhibition is about the so-called outsiders who came to Paris at the beginning of the twentieth century and made their name. For a young artist like Chagall who came from Belarus, Paris must have seemed like a place of infinite opportunity. At the same time, the big city combined with his outsider status must have made Paris feel like an intimidating place, a place where to struggle or to flourish was at the mercy of metropolitan whim, where you could be fêted and spurned in an instant.

When I came to London from the West Country in 1984, I had

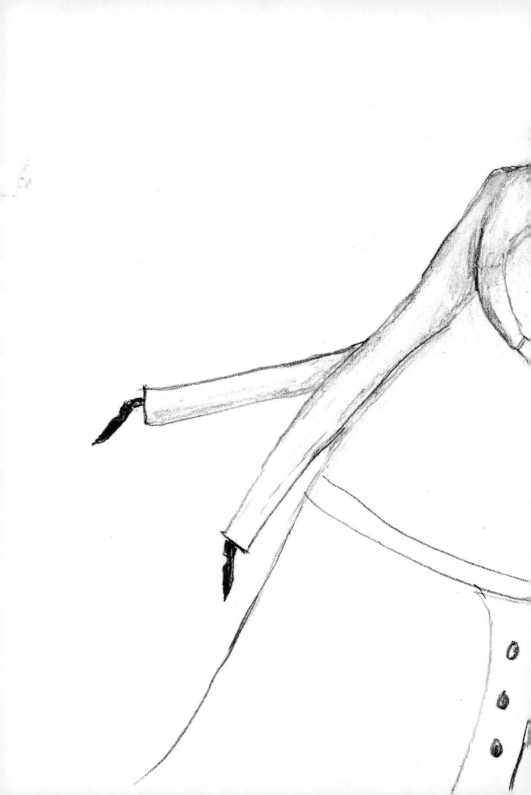

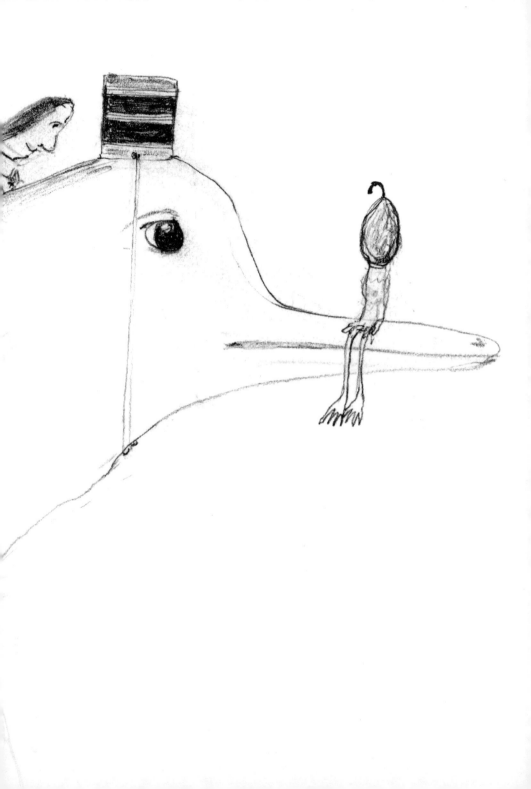

those same thoughts I imagine Chagall had about Paris. London was intimidating and disconcertingly large, and I feared I would never find my way around it. Its size and importance threaten to overwhelm you, to render you insignificant.

But it also felt like you could be anyone you wanted here. That urban indifference is the upside of city living, the anonymity part of the attraction. No one knows you, yet neither do they have any expectation. Your own life here is a blank page waiting to be written on, or an empty stage ready to be walked upon.

As I look at his paintings, I lose myself a bit in Chagall. I always drift off into my own world in galleries; I guess this is due to the communal sense of reverence, and the muted sounds of footfall and appreciation. I usually wander about in a daydream, alone in my thoughts, having become separated from my little group of family and friends.

But there's something else going on here: I feel some strange affinity with these paintings. Other than having felt like an outsider for a bit, I have almost nothing in common with Chagall. I'm not Jewish, I have never been to Belarus. In fact, my only connection with the country is that I used to play my own version of what I imagined their national anthem was – a pompous, speeded-up brass band tune. But I feel very moved.

Why does certain art affect us in this way or that? The stroke of a brush, the huge blocks of colour? Whether delicate, realistic or, quite honestly, baffling?

When we see something of beauty, our brains start making chemicals. Researchers at University College London conducted a series of brain-mapping experiments, where volunteers had their brains scanned while they were shown a series of artworks. The scans revealed that the volunteers had a surge of dopamine, another 'happy' chemical, when they looked at something they considered beautiful, and this reaction was almost instant. Observing art can also reduce cortisol, the so-called stress hormone.

All this de-stressing puts me in a reflective mood. As I stroll back to the hotel in Amsterdam, I recall my first impressions of London, the sprawling strangeness of it, the thrill of getting my first job playing piano in a bar, and I smile at the memory. A near miss with a Dutch cyclist jolts me back to the present. Queuing for a bag of chips and satay sauce at the Vlaams Friteshuis, I'm still thinking about these paintings. Great chips and art, there's a four-word TripAdvisor review of Amsterdam for you.

Sitting outside a bar, dipping the fries into the spicy peanut 'saus', a colonial hangover from the Dutch presence in Indonesia, I am reminded anew why art makes me happy. You can intellectualise it till the cows come home, you can chew over it like a Lakeland terrier with an old slipper, but it never ceases to surprise you. Sometimes all you need to take away from it is the simple aesthetic pleasure that it imparts.

But great art should also be provocative, unsettling even. It wows us with its unfathomable strangeness, but also sometimes catches us off guard with how closely it mirrors our own experience, how it speaks directly to us in our everyday lives. Magical while being disarmingly real, like watching your breath disappear on a cold day, or feeling the sun's warmth on your face.

PERSONAL REFLECTION

11

It's a hot spring day in late April and it feels almost like summer. We are in lockdown due to the coronavirus. The air is drowsy and still with no hint of breeze, and as the heat begins to rise our hens seek out the shady patch of our garden in a hollow under the birch tree. They jostle and bicker and eventually shimmy their backsides into the cool earth to make themselves comfortable, then, suitably ensconced, they doze comically, their red-combed heads drooping, then jerking upright, only to droop once again. The dog snores and inadvertently duets with the drone of bumble bees as these busy themselves over a laburnum flower.

Suddenly a pair of holly blue butterflies bursts over the laurel tree, spinning and fluttering in a frenetic airborne dance of courtship. In an instant the male is sized up, given the once-over and rejected. The female spins away and is gone – zhooom! – over the wall. The

whole drama lasts maybe four seconds. The male flutters about, styles out the knockback, then lands on the laurel, looking a bit crestfallen. He won't have much longer to find a mate and with each rejection his reproductive clock winds down a few more precious minutes. He's pitched on the upper branches, perfectly lit by the sun, his pale underside now visible. I turn to grab my camera but, in that brief moment, he's gone.

I suddenly feel a pang of sympathy for this tiny fragile would-be suitor, and for a minute I am reminded of being sixteen, at the disco, after having being turned down by a girl I asked to dance. This is edge-of-the-seat stuff in my back garden. Butterfly dating! The dozy hens have slept through the whole thing. The dog raises its head from slumber and eyes me cautiously with my camera in hand, then lolls back to sleep.

After this flurry of excitement, I have to calm down with a cup of Earl Grey tea and some low-salt gluten-free rice cakes which have hitherto languished unnoticed at the back of my snack cupboard. As the taste-free, low-fun almost-food sticks to the roof of my mouth, I am struck by how readily the memory of my disco knockback came to mind. At least it was just me who witnessed the holly blue getting mugged off, not a disco full of his mates. I wonder if my memories, unreliable at the best of times, appear more intense due to a heightened sense of awareness elicited by this pandemic. Certainly I've read many news stories of people experiencing extremely vivid dreams during lockdown. Our sleep patterns are all over the place. I had a dream in which I saw everyone I've ever met, while I drank sherry wearing just a towel. Things are not right.

We've all been forced to spend more time with ourselves, in the company of our own thoughts. And I'm thinking that maybe a little more self-awareness and personal reflection is something that we could retain when we come through this. It won't necessarily lead to instant happiness, but it's good training for long-term contentment. And you don't need to leave home, or get on a paddleboard, or a quadbike, or fly a microlite over an active volcano to do it.

According to *Psychology Today*, there are three aspects of awareness that have lasting benefits, and they seem uncannily prescient in identifying how we are coping with these strange times. They are, in no particular order, kindness, a sense of our common humanity, and being more aware of our emotions. All eminently sensible ideas, that could apply to this or any other hardship.

But sometimes I wonder, how can we go back to the way we were after all this? We get to know our neighbours better, having conversations on doorsteps and front paths while socially distancing. We exchange pleasantries from behind masks in the corner shop, like it's a regular thing. But this is far from normal, and underneath I feel uneasy. We don't really know what the long-term effects of this disruption and enforced isolation will be. So we carry on as best we can, trying to stay positive, trying to be productive. We aim for a return to normality, whatever and whenever that may be. A few days later, I find myself standing in the garden, this time awake, unable to sleep in the oppressive heat, drinking sherry and wearing a towel, so the dream was merely a premonition. Normal is still some way off.

As the last mouthful of rice cake absorbs what saliva I have left and dries my mouth to a crisp, I glance up as a sudden movement catches my eye. The female holly blue is back; she's been over the wall and found the grass was not greener, so she's giving our lonely male another shot. He bursts into flight and after a rapid aerial two-step, the new couple take their honeymoon over the chicken shed.

I prise my crispy lips from my teeth, and smile.

Fig. 4 - *Cloud Cupboard*

SWEARING

12

Fig. 5 - *SWEARIMAN saves
a train – but onlookers'
opinion is divided*

I have banged my little toe, again, on the leg of the dining room table. It's a simple wooden table leg, not ornate, and quite visible, so I've got no excuse other than my innate clumsiness. The tabletop is a huge piece of slate which rests unattached atop a wooden framework kept in place purely by its considerable weight. So the table leg does not give an inch. Instantaneously, an untrammelled torrent of garbled profanity erupts from my mouth.

The toe throbs unconscionably, but the swearing makes me feel better.

This is no coincidence. It's not just a psychological trick. It has an actual, physical benefit.

Swearing is good for us, it's been proven. Cursing makes us healthier, and helps us to lead happier, more productive lives. Wtf, Bill, you're just talking bollocks now. No, it's true.

According to a study conducted by Keele University, swearing is not just beneficial as a form of verbal venting, of catharsis. It can actually help you withstand pain. As part of this study, which I have to say sounds like the best fun, participants were asked to submerge their hands in a bowl of iced water, and keep them there for as long as they could stand. During this ~~total hoot~~ ordeal half of the participants were told to repeat a neutral word, and the other half a swear word. I am now picturing a fantastic scenario where one subject sits with her hand in a bowl of ice repeating the word 'curlew' while another lucky participant sits there effing and jeffing. I would pay to watch this it at the Edinburgh Fringe – in fact, I may well have done.

Pain produces a 'fight or flight' response in the body, and it turns out swearing seems to increase stress-related analgesia. The result of the Keele study was unequivocal. The swearers could hold their hands in the bowl 50 per cent longer than the primsters (a word I've just invented for someone who does not, or will not swear).

Using dynamometers, a device like a bike-grip, similar studies revealed that some judicious cursing actually increases grip-strength. Wow. So, swearing makes you more resilient, able to tolerate pain and makes you stronger? I feel the need for a cursing superhero.

According to another study published in the *Journal of Personality Science*, swearing makes you more truthful, the theory being that liars and dissemblers take more time to answer, whereas if you swear, you are exposing your emotions and therefore more likely to be honest.

And yet another article published in *Psychology Today* claims that swearing brings the benefits of increased circulation, elevated endorphins and an overall sense of calm, control and well-being, which you may rightly consider to be some of the key elements for happiness.

For those of you who've attended my stand-up shows, you might recall that I don't really swear during them. It's not a question of morality, or a prissiness about language, or even that I'm a primster. I just revel in the English language, its endless subtlety and variety, and I find that it's quite fit for purpose when it comes to comedy.

But when I bang my toe on the table leg, or trap my finger while assembling a deckchair, or clip my elbow for the umpteenth time on the edge of the car door, then I will give full rein to some imaginative cursing. It's free-form jazz swearing. Words which have hitherto never met become temporary swear-buddies, pressed into service for some incongruous multi-word sweary pile-on.

Although it makes you feel good, and has all manner of health and happiness-giving qualities, it is probably only best to do this in the privacy of your own home. This is my only caveat that whatever benefits swearing confers, these will be on the swearer, not the swearee.

I tried an experiment of my own. I asked my wife to submerge her hand in a bowl of iced water, while I swore indiscriminately to see if that had some bearing on her discomfort. The results were inconclusive, as there was a lot of swearing on both sides and I ended up buying her dinner.

I think it's safe to say, though, that passive swearing just doesn't cut it.

THE UNEXPECTED

13

A chance meeting with an old friend, finding a fiver in the lining of your jacket, winning a whole Dundee cake in a raffle . . . when these sparkling gems of life land in our lap, their unexpected delight makes us happy.

Around 2,500 years ago the Chinese philosopher Zhuangzi wrote *Supreme Happiness*, perhaps the first ever work devoted entirely to the subject. Of course, writing this book means I feel a deep connection with Zhuangzi, as if we are bound together, two points on an endless continuum, so I was intrigued to know what he had to say.

Supreme Happiness aims to divine the nature of happiness – no mean feat – and to do this Zhuangzi favours embracing the mysterious side of life – the unexpected.

His advice is not to dwell on whether events are good or bad, but to just inhabit the moment, embrace 'the way of nature' and 'dwell in its unity'. This sounds great and I'm sure we'd all love to just contemplate a bumblebee in the tranquillity of the forest, or dwell in nature's unity, but this won't get the dishwasher fixed.

I admire his attitude, and perhaps in China 2,500 years ago, the idea of 'inhabiting the moment' was radical, even revolutionary. Today, though, this sounds like exactly the kind of vague piffle that has spawned a multibillion-dollar happiness industry. If you've ever been on a windy beach, struggling to assemble a buggy while a toddler has a meltdown, and the dog's cocked its leg on someone else's picnic, inhabiting the moment is not something that springs to mind.

But Zhuangzi was clearly onto something in his advocacy of the unexpected, as this is a strand of happiness that seems to have endured over the centuries.

From around 1500, happiness became associated with the meaning we ascribe to it today, namely good luck, success and

contentment. After all, 'happiness' comes from the Old Norse word 'happ', meaning 'luck' or 'chance'. This was the case until 1725, when Francis Hutcheson, an Irish reverend and philosopher, wrote a treatise catchily titled *An Inquiry into the Original of Our Ideas of Beauty and Virtue*. Hutcheson posited the idea that happiness should be less about gratification and pleasure, and more about civic responsibility. So basically, stop eating crisps and pushing your mate into a hedge

Fig. 6 - *Bald viking finds gold coin in his helmet*

for a laugh, and help out a bit. This was a less indulgent version of happiness, which influenced the writers of the eighteenth century, including those who drew up the Declaration of Independence.

The famous phrase 'Life, liberty and the pursuit of happiness' was not an invitation to crack open the sherry and play pin the tail on the donkey until the police are called, but rather the more sober pursuit of duty and contentment, finding a meaningful role and a sense of purpose. Since then, I imagine, the decline in the usage of that phrase has mirrored the fact that happiness has come to mean hedonism, pleasure, fun, enjoyment.

The word happiness reached peak usage in 1803, and was thereafter in steady decline, reaching an all-time low in 1988.

I don't know why 1803 particularly prompted the word 'happiness' to be bandied about so much, although perhaps the reason here in Britain was that we were at war with France. It might have been due to the opening of the Surrey Iron Railway, the first public railway between Wandsworth and Croydon, meaning that Croydon was now opened up to bring families together. 'Oh, Aunt Agatha lives in Croydon, and now we shall see her most every week, oh, happiness unbound!' said the advertisement, I imagine.

And perhaps 1988 was a turning point for happiness. As this shiny hollow decade of unbridled materialism, big hair and partying neared its end, there were strikes and unrest. The world was maybe poised to turn a corner and rediscover a more meaningful kind of happy. It seems that way, as since the late eighties the word happiness is enjoying a resurgence and is again on an upward curve.

Our lives are full of wishing luck and superstition. Rituals, numbers, traditions are found in every culture on the planet. I am not a betting man, but once I couldn't help but abide by Zhuangzi's doctrine and go with the flow. I was on the phone and during the conversation, I said the phrase 'blessing in disguise'. As I said the words, the exact same phrase was spoken on television by the commentator, referring to a horse: '. . . and in the 3.45, at 14 to 1, Blessing in Disguise.' It was as if I had lip-synced it. A sign surely! Time to inhabit the moment. It was 3.35 in the afternoon, so I cut the phone call short, and immediately went to the betting shop in my street. All I had on me was a fiver, which I'd found under a piece of Dundee cake. 'Five pounds on Blessing in Disguise, please.' 'To win?' 'Of course, to win!'

I must have exuded such naive yet credible confidence that a few of the grey-faced betting shop regulars sidled up and placed a similar bet. I stood and watched the race, my face beaming with the delight of an utter novice, my once-in-a-blue-moon flutter. I knew the horse would win, I had just been given a clear message from the 'Dao' of horse racing, the god of good fortune. I was subjecting to 'the way of nature'. I had been shown the future – just a glimpse of it.

And sure enough, Blessing in Disguise romped home the winner by two lengths.

I took my £75 and I could lie and say I started a foundation for lonely pheasants, but I didn't. I bought some new hiking socks and with the remainder I took my wife out for dinner, and we toasted our blessing.

PLAYING THE GAMELAN

14

I am in the back seat of a cramped taxi as we thread our way through the network of narrow roads that criss-cross the villages of Northern Bali. A little flock of white egret fly in a perfect V formation over the rice fields. Water buffalo help to plough new furrows for the rice planting, wrangled by conical-hat-wearing Balinese, forming a tableau that could be a scene from history. We are en route to meet a craftsman, a maker of musical instruments. Specifically, a xylophone-type instrument, part of the gamelan series of instruments which originated in Indonesia and consist usually of metal bars, or chimes, which are struck with little curved mallets.

The versions of gamelan vary through the archipelago. The Javanese version is slower, stately, even austere-sounding compared to the much more exuberant, frenetic Balinese incarnation. I'm on my way to try out one of the Balinese gamelan instruments, akin to

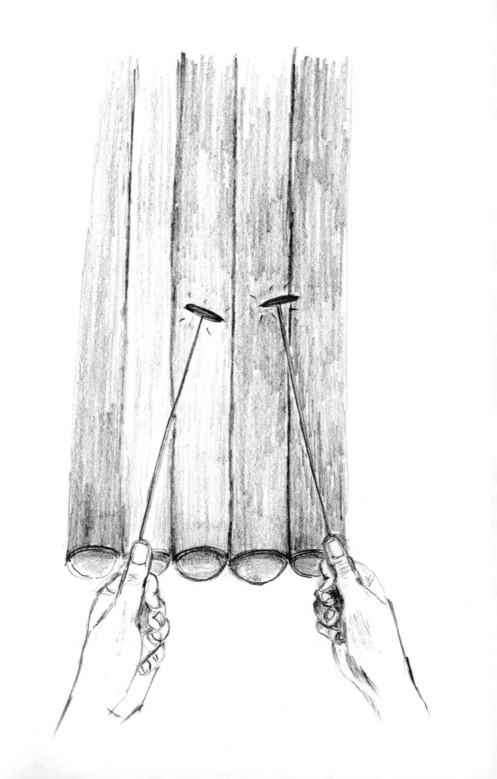

a marimba, made from tubes of bamboo slung with string from a bamboo frame. To play a note, the tubes are struck with thin, whippy beaters, again made from bamboo, tipped with rubber ends formed from car tyres. This homemade instrument is known as a *rindik*, and this craftsman, Wayan, is a master.

The first evidence of a musical ensemble is seen on the bas-relief of the eighth-century Buddhist temple in Borobudur, on the island of Java. Once with my wife and toddler son, we climbed this beautiful monument at dawn to reach the bell-shaped *stupas* at the top. Borobudur is not just a beautiful stone temple, it's also a teaching aid in the form of an introduction to Buddhism. The carvings on the walls as you climb the steps to the top depict Buddha's own ascent to enlightenment. His temptation and indulgence of the many Earthly pleasures occupy the lower sections. As you near the top, the carvings begin to disappear, eventually giving way to smooth stone representing Buddha's final enlightenment, his journey beyond distraction and temptation, to arrive at only calm and blank serenity.

A party of school children are already at the top and, seeing a Western family, approach us with questions and to try out their English. A girl wearing a headscarf and holding a pad of paper asks me politely where we are from, and then asks me a question of such profound simplicity I struggle to answer. 'What are the crops in your country?' Crops? I am stumped. Er . . . wheat? Turnips? I dunno. I formulate a sentence in my head along the lines of 'due to modernisation, much of our agriculture is highly mechanised and situated a long way from residential areas, so we have little or no contact with farming, and in fact the occasions when we are more connected to growers and farmers is a source of happiness, but for now this rural slash urban dissonance is a low-level buzz of anxiety that interferes with our daily equanimity.' But it comes out differently. 'We live in the city so we get our food from the supermarket,' I parp out like some strange simulated human. I am not sounding convincing, least of all to myself, so they edge away. 'Thank you!' Yeah, thanks for nothin'.

The gamelan is, to me, so fascinating because it doesn't adhere to Western musical modes, and perhaps because of that we react to it in a different way. We have become familiar with a form, a structure to Western music which most of our classical music tends to adhere to. It has an introduction, an overture, a theme, a development, a conclusion. Our pop music also often has a pattern to it, a verse chorus structure.

Gamelan is more about creating an atmosphere. There's no real intro, or middle section, or end; there are just waves of intensity. At some points, the playing recedes to just one solitary chiming beat, then it gradually builds up again, and complex rhythms and harmonies start to materialise.

Another feature of the gamelan is that it doesn't conform to Western scales; it follows a seven-note or septatonic scale. This allows those with no musical training to get a passable tune out of it. And not only that, because a family of gamelan are all tuned to each other, you can happily clang away with a mallet and not sound out of place.

There's no expectation for a song structure, no conclusion, you just tune into a group of interconnected sounds, and find that after a short time you can contribute meaningfully.

This is why I love the gamelan orchestra. The simplicity of it belies the beauty and hypnotic effect of the long rounds of music that flow from it. There's something ancient about it that feels at once familiar, an echo perhaps of our first attempts at communal music making, immortalised in a temple carving.

The taxi pulled into Wayan's compound, and a man of indeterminate age with an impressive shock of black hair, wearing a purple batik shirt and sarong, appeared in the bright sun. Wayan - for it was he - was initially wary, but after a few words of introduction he brought some eye-wateringly sweet orange squash and some rice crackers. He seemed keen to know more about me. I prayed silently he wouldn't ask me about crops. He asked what I did for a living. Here, at least, I had an answer.

'Pelawat!' I grinned. 'Orang lucu!' He immediately burst out laughing. Which, when you tell someone you're a comedian, a 'funny man', is always a good start.

He led me over to a raised platform, shaded from the sun by a roof thatched with *alang alang*, on which were placed two *rindik*. We sat cross-legged at each while Wayan effortlessly made this homemade instrument sing with rhythm and seven-tone harmony. The rippling marimba sounds filled the motionless air while the cicada's chorus rose and fell with this intoxicating soundtrack.

'You!' he suddenly stopped and thrust a pair of beaters into my hand.

He swivelled back round to his instrument, resumed playing and immediately created a simple lilting pattern of woodily plaintive notes. I tentatively joined in, trying to match the rhythm and create harmonies to his flow.

I don't quite know how long I was there. The cascade of notes flowed over the smooth matting of the shaded *bale* in which we sat, and out into the compound. While the taxi driver snoozed, iridescent butterflies fluttered lazily around my head as I inhaled the sweet scent of frangipani. The music ebbed and flowed. More sweet squash was called for. Time became irrelevant and I experienced either a massive sugar rush, or a moment of pure happiness.

LAUGHING

15

Because I'm a comedian, people often ask me, 'How do you think up jokes?' My answer is always the same: 'I start with a laugh and work backwards.' Hahaha?

For me, laughter is a pure form of happiness, because it's raw, unadulterated and you can't control it. It can just turn up unannounced and completely transform how you are feeling. We laugh despite ourselves, as if laughter is no respecter of how we ought to be, or think, or behave. It's pure happiness precisely because there's no way to predict it.

As an asthmatic, I've never subscribed to the old saying that laughter is the best medicine. If it's a straight choice between laughing and using an inhaler, I'm going with the inhaler every time. I am, though, genuinely amazed by what I'm told are the health benefits of laughing. This peculiar activity decreases stress hormones and increases immune cells. Laughing improves your ability to resist disease! It even reduces pain levels over time. If this is true, and jokes are just homeopathic prescriptions in linguistic form, maybe there's some merit after all in pursuing this low-rent and reckless endeavour. On my passport where it says 'occupation', I might cross out 'comedian' and write 'holistic healer'. On my business card it might say, 'I can relieve lumbago with whimsy and sarcasm.'

Of course, some people might prefer to pursue laughter's health-

92

giving quality by choosing to do laughter yoga instead. I'm not sure I approve of this form of exercise that borrows from my chosen path. I am sure it's marvellous, but when I hear about this kind of thing, I just think, *Well, those are laughs I could have had. Instead of jokes, you've wasted your laughs on yoga.* But then I would think that.

I once read about an experiment which discovered that rats have the ability to laugh. It made me wonder, what do rats find funny? Is it stories about what idiots voles are? Or how mice are just so gullible? Or do they prefer long-form stories that subvert the rat narrative? Or darker stuff about the plague, or surreal stream of consciousness ranting, or just gifs of other rats falling off drainpipes?

And then I thought, this is just another form of pressure for us human comics: interspecies laughs. We pride ourselves that our comedy works anywhere, but this presents us with a new challenge, and opens the door to a potentially crushing review: 'He couldn't even make a rat laugh.'

I find all kinds of things funny. Like the films of the taciturn Finn Aki Kaurismäki that are so unremittingly bleak, where there is often no hope, and the characters lurch from one setback to another. Yet the more hopeless their situation, the more troubles heaped on their heads, the more we laugh.

Laughter brings about a feeling of kinship, of togetherness. I'd like to imagine it's what bonded our ancestors together, helped to create strong friendships and family groups. I am not suggesting that our Neolithic forebears staged open mike nights: 'Next up, its Og the Uneasy! Give 'im a chance!' But there must have been a moment when one of them slipped on the ice, or walked into a tree, or dropped a rock on his foot and the whole tribe fell about.

I'm also intrigued as to when sarcasm first happened.

Commenting on another's simplistic cave drawings, one hunter might have said, 'These crude scratchings are so realistic; omigod, it's like I'm there, on the hunt.'

'Aw, thanks.'

'I was being sarcastic.'

'What's that?'

'I don't know, but I like it.'

Over the years, I have heard all manner of different laughs emanate from an audience. The cackle, the explosive snort, the repressed squeak followed by a high-pitched wheeze, the involuntary whinny, the breathless rasp, the belly-laugh . . . the full sonic range of human glee. Laughter is good for us. It's a release, a stress-reliever; it causes the brain to release endorphins that help to reduce pain and trigger positive feelings.

It inhibits the stress hormone cortisol, and stimulates the hippocampus, the brain's memory centre.

Which is why so many of our fondest memories involve laughter. Once when my wife and I were arguing about something, and I can't even remember what, I stubbed my toe on the kitchen table, causing me to yelp like a dog, leap into the air, and let loose a volley of incoherent cursing.

Our cockatoo, Molly, who had been sitting on her perch throughout the ding-dong, suddenly burst out laughing. Proper, human-sounding mocking laughter. She bobbed and weaved on the perch in a paroxysm of hilarity.

Suddenly, our argument evaporated. We were so struck by the timing, the tone and the perfect incongruity of the moment, we both burst out laughing.

So maybe interspecies laughter is possible, after all.

Fig. 7 - *'It sounds like a cackle'*

EQUATIONS

16

In 2015, I reached the milestone of a half-century on Earth. It seemed to be as good a time as any to take stock a bit, to allow myself the luxury of a brief glance back. When you're climbing a volcano, there's no point pausing to take in the view until you've got to a decent height.

I was writing a stand-up show at the time, considering, among other subjects, the nature of happiness.

I was intrigued to read an article whereby some scientists claimed to have found an actual equation for happiness. This brought back uncomfortable memories of school maths lessons where equations had made me feel anxious and a bit hot round the temples, and this one was no different. I could tell you what it is, but that's not really the point. It's just another variation of the high-sounding concepts and affirmations like 'the soul of now', 'owning your moment', 'you are still the person you will be in a couple of minutes' and other unconscionable twaddle that means that the 'get happy' gravy train is a monster of an industry worth $11 billion in America alone.

The received wisdom is that the world has become an uncertain place of endless turmoil and this leads us to worry more and seek out easily digestible solutions, hence these 'equations' for happiness. But hasn't the world always been a place of endless turmoil, and what has changed is the technology to make us more aware of it?

When Krakatoa erupted in 1883, the sound of the explosion was

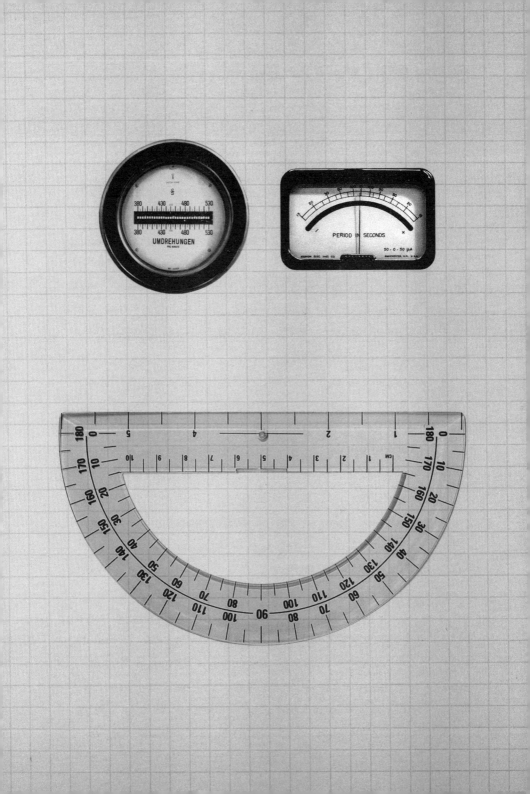

heard thousands of miles away, and the immense ash cloud drifted around the world, causing brilliant sunsets for months after. But this cataclysmic event sent shock waves in an altogether different way. For most people at that time, international events seemed distant and vague. Knowledge of scandal and disaster was limited to the town, the village, even the street you lived in. Because this was a global catastrophe, it made the headlines in countries around the world, and it's perceived as the first truly worldwide news event.

These days, the unblinking glare of the internet serves us an endless buffet of peril and death, which I think skews our perception of disaster so unconsciously we end up in a constant state of low-level anxiousness. The heart-rending and downright depressing stories about the world are

served up side by side with some lightweight showbiz flummery. War, famine, genocide competing for your attention with celebrity gossip.

The natural reaction to this is a combination of outrage, horror and disapproval. But constant changes of emotional gear become wearying so eventually, worn out by our eyebrows going up and down and a tongue ulcer brought on by excessive tutting, our reactions become dulled. News is reduced to the white noise of unprocessed information, unfiltered raw data, what Germaine Greer calls the 'unsynthesised manifold'.

As a corrective to trying to work out an appropriate response to complex issues, I've come up with my own equation for happiness.

I was camping with my son on the South Downs. We set up the tent, and built a fire. We played ping-pong on the outdoor table provided, a reliable guarantee of fun. Over a camping stove we cooked up some sausages and ate them in a soft roll while we perched awkwardly on a slightly sloping tree stump as a tawny owl hooted its approval. Sausage + roll + owl = contentment. So nearly there.

As if we were now part of some Enid Blyton adventure, we then set off into the woods to whittle sticks and carve our names in trees, and generally be at one with the woodland.

Back at the camp, and I realised that somehow my car keys had fallen out of my pocket. Our mood refused to be dampened, and we immediately retraced our steps, going back and forth along the trail like bloodhounds till we found them. We danced about high-fiving in the woods, crashing about in the bracken like demented weasels.

So here's an equation for you: being outdoors + campfire + sausage in a roll ÷ finding your car keys = happiness

PADDLEBOARDING

17

I am floating downstream on the River Thames, standing upright, with knees slightly bent, atop what looks like a long surfboard. You can't see from the shore, but I am smiling from ear to ear at the board's quiet progress over the sunlit water, the company of ducks, the way the paddle rests lightly in my hands, the pull of its blade trailing in the water to keep my balance. As I direct my gaze at the pale cabbage-white sun, low in the milky Tupperware sky, a heron flaps stiffly overhead.

I'm wearing an assortment of mismatched clothing. Trainers, running leggings, some cycling shorts, a long-sleeved surfing top, a buoyancy aid and, of course, a Santa hat. This is my Christmas paddleboard with a flotilla of similarly attired individuals as we make our way down the Thames from Kew to Putney. Our launch point was an old draw-dock by Kew Bridge and now the ebb tide nudges us downstream, gently assisting each paddle stroke.

Our curious fleet of waterborne oddballs easily outstrips those determined souls who are braving the chill along the riverbanks. Out here, though, in midstream, their conversations are muted, and we occupy our own bubble of sound. Through my feet, I can feel the board vibrate slightly as the light breeze creates a little surface chop that slaps and gurgles along the underside.

Stand-up paddleboarding, to give it its full title, or SUP, is generally thought to have begun in Hawaii in the 1950s. A surfer, tiring perhaps and wishing to catch some last waves at the end of the day, grabbed a boat oar to give his board some extra power as he paddled out over the surf.

These days, paddleboarders are a familiar sight on most surf beaches and on any stretch of water from lakes, rivers and canals to estuaries and coastal inlets.

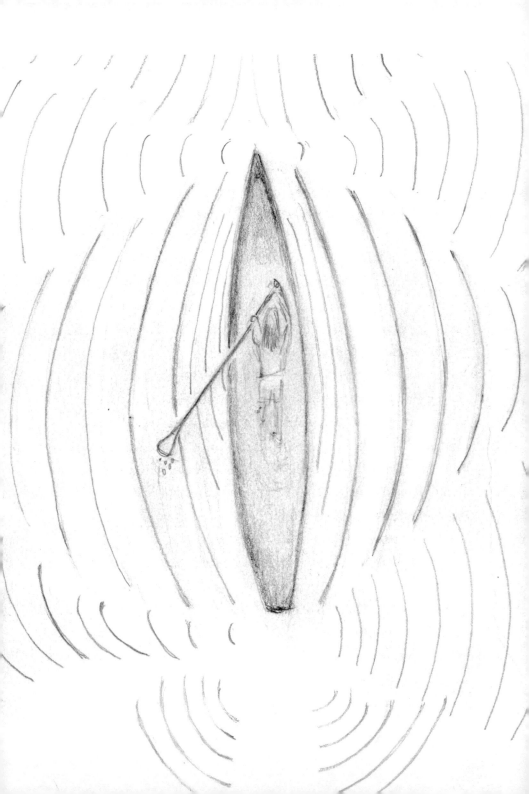

Paddling upright on any stretch of water requires a level of concentration that helps to zone out intrusive thoughts. There are other significant health benefits. The mere act of balancing engages all manner of muscles, including that which we hear about repeatedly at the gym, the 'core'. I once was assigned a personal trainer for one free session when I applied for a new gym membership. She was lean and angular, resembling an Olympic gymnast, and told me very sternly that she was going to 'challenge my core'. Over the course of the next few minutes, I didn't feel that it was just my untoned midriff that was being challenged, but my sense of self, who I was and what I was doing with my life. Why are we here? Is there an afterlife? My mind started to drift to other abstract questions: why couldn't my arms be a bit longer? If I lie down next to the bathroom scales, could I weigh my own head?

As I was saying, SUP has been around a while, but as I discovered, a lot longer than you'd think. I was once on a trip down to the far south of Tasmania, to Melaleuca. This is an extraordinary place, remote and stunningly beautiful, a place of pristine wilderness, mirror-calm lakes and unyielding bush. It's home also to one of the oldest aboriginal communities, the Needwonnee people, and evidence of their traditional coastal life remains in huge piles of shells.

Walking in near silence on boardwalks surrounded by button grass one day, we diverted down a side path, which led to a promontory that extended into the lake. And there on the jetty was something ancient but at the same time familiar: an aboriginal raft made from tree bark, in the exact size and dimensions of my paddleboard.

This, I realised, must have been a forty thousand-year-old paddleboard, surely among the world's first. An aboriginal fisherman must have picked up his paddle and slid the bark vessel silently into the limpid water.

'Where are you going?' 'Just off to challenge my core.'

Back on the Thames, as we arrive at our destination – the slipway at Putney – the long rays of the sun ignite the odd starburst on the water, and reflect on the London-bricked banks.

Stand-up paddleboarding is something that looks hard, but is in fact surprisingly easy once you get the hang of it, but you still need to be fairly fit to enjoy it. New paddlers are often taken aback by how much of a workout it is. Certainly it's more fun than being in the gym, hefting weights or jogging with a phone strapped to your arm.

SUP challenges your core but without the accompanying self-doubt. It's been strengthening our central muscles for centuries. All you need is a stretch of water, a board and a sense of balance.

It is joyous. It feels right. That's it! It actually feels like we are meant to do this as humans.

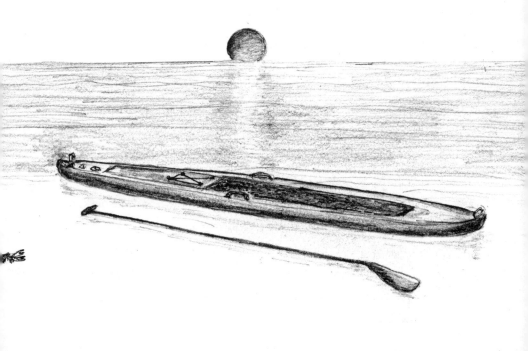

READING

18

For the avoidance of doubt, I am writing about reading, as in 'interpreting the written word with your eyes or, if blind, fingers', not Reading, the town in Berkshire. Which is not to say that Reading has not been a source of happiness. Indeed, I have spent many happy times there, performing at the Reading Festival and at the Hexagon Theatre in ~~the Concrete Underworld of Despair~~ Queen's Walk.

There are days when we have the time and the need to lose ourselves in a book. I consume books and the written word like homemade brownies; I revel in being gripped by the twists and turns of a thriller, being immersed in a classic or a biography, fascinated by a feature, a column, even the instructions that accompany a vegetable steamer.

There are many scholarly articles which list the benefits of reading, ranging from having a greater vocabulary to being more thoughtful towards others, or even broadening your outlook on life generally. Novels in particular can allow you to visualise and imagine scenarios you might find yourself in, so that you rehearse how you might react to those situations in real life. The opportunity to live and work aboard a wooden Nantucket whaling ship has probably now passed, but you can feel the salty air and the deck under your feet when you read *Moby Dick*.

I began rereading Herman Melville's classic around the time the Norwegian author Karl Ove Knausgaard's autobiographical books were causing a sensation. The series entitled 'My Struggle' charts his life in forensic, minute detail. When his mother gives the young Karl a bowl of soup, he describes the weight of the bowl, the steam coming from it, the shape of the spoon, the table on which he places the soup. . . *Moby Dick* is magnificently descriptive, and detailed also, but the difference is the flourish, the turn of phrase that stays with you. Knausgaard being amazed that his father had some sixth sense of his arrival, then only later realising it was his footfall on the gravel that had alerted him, is typical of the writer's fine detail and dive into memory, but it's Melville's description of a whalers' graveyard that has stayed with me over the years: 'Faith, like a jackal, hunts among the tombs.'

Sometimes reading is just escapism, which is also fine. Read the classics, sure, but also an occasional lightweight airport pulp novel is a good palate cleanser for denser, richer fare. I was once stuck on a fourteen-hour layover in Indonesia on the island of Sulawesi, in the hot and crowded airport of Makassar. At the small bookshop, I browsed the carousel and found only two books printed in English: Stephen Hawking's *A Brief History of Time* and Tom Clancy's *Patriot Games*. I decided to buy them both, and I ended up reading them as I sat for hours on a bucket-shaped plastic seat bolted to the floor.

They were both entertaining in equal measure. Hawking for the grand, sweeping scope of his vision, the sometimes impenetrable language and the linear style, which makes it a tough read at the best of times; Clancy for the terse, peremptory dialogue, detailed descriptions of ordnance, and the occasional outbursts of violence with high-calibre weaponry. But then I would say that, as they were all I had to keep me occupied, along with tasty plates of nasi campur, egg sambal and beef rendang.

My most vivid reading memories are those where the place I was in at the time was not my usual run-of-the-mill kind of environment. Before I travelled around Colombia with my friend Sean, I was looking for a book, something a bit different, something that might sustain me in an unfamiliar place. My choice was *Vineland* by Thomas Pynchon, a mind-boggling, hallucinatory novel of lurid characters in surreal tableaus, set against a backdrop of an examination of American

Fig. 8 - *Another lost bestseller*

counter culture. Its memory lived with me long after I got back to London, and it remains one of my favourite travelling companions. The characters and scenarios seemed to project outwards in glorious technicolour in ever more strange and unsettling ways, which exactly matched the experience we had trekking through the northern jungles of Colombia to the Lost City.

At dawn I wandered among the market stalls of Santa Marta on Colombia's Caribbean coast, sipping a tiny paper cup of the strongest coffee I have ever tasted. All around was a whirl of activity and colour. I felt detached from this scene yet also completely immersed, a curious sensation of being an observer and at the same time a participant. This book made me feel that also. I knew next to nothing about American infiltration of counter culture groups by CIA operatives and alternative postal services in the 1960s, but I was wrapped up in the story nonetheless. No book I think before or since has so captured my mood and experience, and replicated the moment I was living in.

We trekked through the jungles of Colombia, spent many weeks in the country. All the possessions I had then are now gone, jettisoned en route, at the charity shop or simply vanished. The backpack didn't make it to the end of the trek, and we donated some of our clothes to our guides, but the book somehow survived, and now sits on my shelf, travelling days over. Did I really heft it halfway round the world, to the Lost City, La Ciudad Perdida?

A dark coffee stain on the cover says that I did.

TREES

I am not averse to hugging a tree, but I prefer not to do so just outside my house. It's a very personal and slightly awkward act that I'd feel self-conscious doing in front of a Deliveroo driver. In the privacy of a forest, though, I'll hug away like the next man.

Once, on a walk in a meadow on a hot summer's day, the path I was on gave way to a dark pine forest. There was an immediate feeling of cosiness in the shade. It was cooler, and the bright afternoon sun only permeated here and there, causing the forest floor to appear randomly spotlit.

As I walked through the trees, I glanced left and right. As this was a planted pine forest, the trees were aligned in neat rows, so my view changed in an orderly

19

way. With one stride all the trees lined up, and I had an uninterrupted view deep into the forest; with the next, they slipped out of alignment, causing graph-like patterns to form that curved away in a pleasing arc. A goldcrest plinked about in the canopy.

In 2006, a study conducted among young adults in Poland in which some participants were asked to gaze for fifteen minutes at a winter forest while others stared at a treeless urban landscape produced interesting results. Those who looked at the winter forest were more relaxed by the end of the session. The interesting twist is that the forest was without leaves and greenery, which suggested that even short exposure to a barren forest imparted a substantially better emotional, restorative and revitalising effect on the participants than a cityscape.

First developed in the 1980s, the idea of 'shinrin-yoku' or 'forest bathing' became government policy in Japan after a seminal study, where around six hundred participants were asked to record their mood during urban and forest walks for fifteen minutes (again). The study showed that those who walked in urban areas recorded more feelings of stress and anxiety than those who walked through a forest. Translated literally as 'absorbing the atmosphere of the forest', 'shinrin-yoku' was adopted as a national health programme. We are playing catch-up here in the UK, but there are now centres of shinrin-yoku around Britain.

Trees simply make us feel good, in a way that doesn't require much thought. In fact, we're not even aware of the good they're doing half the time. Never mind the reduced stress and the sense of tranquillity – the *ataraxia*, as the Greeks have it. There's the aroma, the essential oils they give off that have been proven to soothe our city-frazzled minds with a dose of arboreal nurture. Their age, their connection with the past, the wildlife that they support, and of course the tactile pleasure they impart all contribute to making us happy.

Back in my forest, I am sufficiently isolated now to get hold of a tree. The sap is heady in my nostrils, the ground softened by pine needles. I wrap my arms around the trunk of a fine specimen and lean in for a hug. I feel the rough texture of the bark under my fingers, and against my cheek. I briefly close my eyes.

A couple of hikers appear out of nowhere.

'All right, Bill!'

I jump out of my skin, half stumbling back from the pine-fresh hug.

'Always had you down as a tree-hugger!'

They stomp off along the trail.

As I write this on a late May evening, trees are featuring heavily in my lockdown sensory enjoyment. In so-called normal times, there would be many more layers to my neighbourhood soundtrack, a deal more cars' engines roaring, television chatter, dogs barking, and the evening burble of conversation and laughter from outside the pub on the corner. Tonight, I've heard nothing except the sound of the wind in the trees. Earlier a fusillade of swifts hurtled over the house, their screaming calls pinballing around the rooftops. Now even the swifts are silent so just the light wind remains, and the trees make the only sound.

I am reminded of the German poet and philosopher, Hermann Hesse's words:

'When we have learned to listen to trees, that is home . . . that is happiness.'

CONFRONTING YOUR FEARS
(PART 1)

20

I am sitting bunched up awkwardly in a cramped single-engine aircraft that is gradually ascending in wide looping turns over the Gold Coast of Australia. The ground has quickly receded enough to reveal the arc of the coastline and now the Earth's curvature itself. The sun beats down from a cloudless sky, making this perfect skydiving weather, and from my window I marvel and quail in equal measure at the glittering expanse of ocean stretching away to the east.

Suddenly I begin to feel butterflies in my stomach – well, more like giant cicadas. I'd agreed to do this for my son's sake who was gung-ho super keen to try it, but I realise I am not entirely sure how I will react when the moment to jump arrives. Maybe I'll just freeze, then what? This must have happened before, right? People must sometimes lose their bravado and change their minds, and what then? Do the instructors abort the jump, return to the airfield? Or do they just dart you with a tranq gun and jump with you anyway? Maybe that's why they're wearing helmets and goggles, to protect themselves from the drool, which will fly upwards out of my open mouth as I hurtle down in slack-jawed earthbound slumber?

I fight down these thoughts as the cicadas of unease continue to flutter, and focus on staying calm. But it's hard when you can hear your heart thumping in your chest. I made the mistake of getting into the plane last, thinking this way, I can watch my son and the others jump out, and if I freeze, at least I'm not holding anyone up. But this backfired immediately as once inside we all turned around to face the back of the plane, so I'm going to be first out.

The instructors are all hyped and pumped, as of course you would be if you did this all day, every day. I had talked to Pete, my instructor, briefly on the ground as we were gearing up. He seemed nice. Confident. Upbeat. That's all you want in a skydiving buddy:

straightforwardly happy. No one wants them to be moody or introspective. If he was, he wasn't showing it.

And then suddenly, without warning, the aircraft's door is slid open. The noise of the air rushing past fills the cramped cabin with deafening immediacy. It's extraordinarily unnerving, an open door on a plane. It's wrong! It's now horribly real and ridiculous, and I am suddenly laughing in a slightly hysterical way. Of course, of course you open the door. How else did you think this would work, Bill? I don't know, I hadn't thought that far ahead, I thought perhaps that the floor of the plane would just open out like bomb doors, and the instructors wouldn't tell you when that would happen, and you'd be released that way – surprise! – which would somehow make it all more bearable.

I am now confronted with a scenario which elicits a strong survival instinct. Every fibre of my being is screaming, 'NO! What are you doing?? The plane door is open!!' Instead, Pete tells me to shuffle forwards towards the door. Now he instructs me to sit on the edge of the open doorway, put my legs out of the plane, and dangle them down onto the fuselage. Suddenly I am about five years old, sitting on a stone wall, my calves brushing against the barnacles that cover the rough sea wall, overlooking a Pembrokeshire beach while dangling my spindly legs over the sand, which is about a foot below. My mother is handing me an ice cream. I recall this as vividly as what I see before me: the distant outline of the coast, the ocean, and a lot of sky.

A voice cuts through my Welsh holiday memory, and the tattooed hand of Pete the Aussie taps me on the arm.

'Cross yer arms, mate, then I'll count down from three, then we go. Wait till I tap you on the shoulder, then uncross yer arms, put them out front and yer legs back as far as ya can,' he shouts over the rushing wind.

I nod manically. I am also conscious that this madness is being filmed from every angle: Pete has a GoPro camera on his wrist; another instructor will jump a split second before us to capture the whole thing. Always thinking of the shot, I start smiling like a loon as I do what he says, and with my arms crossed over my chest I imagine I resemble some cackling pharaoh.

'OK, three.'

My heart begins beating at some hitherto unknown rate.

'Two.'

Pulse now the same speed as the propeller.

'One.'

Time stands still. Pete shoves us both out of the plane. Wooooahh!! My whole consciousness shuts down and reboots again in one second.

And then I just feel incredible exhilaration. Flight! Well, falling from a great height. The pull of gravity is giddying, the speed and velocity mind-draining. An adrenaline rush like nothing on Earth. I've rocked out at Wembley Arena, I've played cowbells with Deep Purple at the Albert Hall, I've been grilled mercilessly on *Loose Women*, but this is the next level.

This is not just about the act of flinging yourself from a light aircraft at fifteen thousand feet.

It's about overcoming fear. Conquering fear. Confronting fear, looking it in the eye, and not backing down, until fear blinks first.

As you glide towards the Earth, and finally touch down, the feeling of achievement is huge; the beam on your face and the swagger is something else.

I have to confess that the inclusion of skydiving here in this book is due to my determination to write only from actual experience.

Empirical research in the name of truth! To be honest, I have always been a little resistant to these kind of gung-ho thrill-seeking activities or one of those '100 things to do' type lists as a way to achieve happiness. They always seemed too brief, too transitory to really impart any lasting contentment. I've always thought those 'things to do' ought to be less instantly gratifying, more lifelong sustaining experiences, like learning a language, or having a modicum of self-perception, both of which I include elsewhere in the book.

But having tested gravity and found it's working fine, I reckon that the effects are not just transitory, they are long-lasting, perhaps even life-changing. Yes, it was a gung-ho, thrill-seeking ding-dong that was all over by half past nine in the morning, but I feel changed, subtly different. I feel I could do anything, within reason, and with a harness, and a safety chat.

Even give *Loose Women* another try.

DOGS

21

I am trying to coax one of our dogs, Tiger, off the bed so I can lie on it.

He's a large, ungainly bag of bones, half greyhound, half Indonesian street dog. He is a rescue case, so when we first got him I put up with this nonsense as I felt sorry for him. 'He's had a hard life,' I would say, 'he's making up for the years of sleeping rough on the streets.' Now, after many years of doggie comfort, healthy food, exercise and love, this sympathy act he pulls is wearing a bit thin.

I look directly at him, jerk my thumb in the direction of the bedroom door, and say, firmly, 'Out!' He cocks his head in mock incomprehension, looks around as if I might be speaking to someone else, but otherwise there's not a flicker of movement.

Time for the secret weapon. For some reason, he dislikes cameras and phones. I don't know why, it's one of those odd quirks you discover with rescue animals. Anyway, it's a sure-fire way of getting him to move. I pull out my phone and start snapping away. As soon as he hears the sound of photos being taken, his lanky frame starts to stir; he draws himself up, stretches and totters off in a huff.

I am constantly deleting dozens of out-of-focus photos of Tiger which commonly feature the back of his head, his tail or a backwards resentful glance. Why do we put ourselves through all this for these creatures? Is it their wagging tails? Their dopey slobbering faces? Their constant capacity for public embarrassment?

We are all well aware by now of how they've been our pals for thousands of years, how they offer us love, unconditionally, how they seem to be empathetic and read our moods, and so much more. You have to be out in all weathers walking the dog, so pet owners tend to be more physically fit and are generally more socially outgoing. I've never been out with dogs yet and not had a chat with some other dog owner. All this has positive knock-on effects that can counteract loneliness and even boost your self-esteem.

Many studies will tell you this, and that's all marvellous, but what they don't mention is that you'll have dog hair on your clothes and poo-bags in the pocket of every coat you own. A dog treat will get mixed up with your loose change, which will raise eyebrows with other shoppers at the twenty-four-hour garage when it appears you're trying to pay for an ice cream with a dog biscuit.

'Saw that Bill Bailey up the garage, trying to buy a Magnum with a Bonio. He's losing it,' said 'a source'.

The thing I love about dogs is that you get so much back from them – if you put the hours in, they repay you threefold. Not so much the praying mantis we had for a while. Every night I'd talk to him, tell him about my day, maybe sing a selection of eighties hits to him. He just stared indifferently at me from within his glass tank.

For some reason or other, we had a few giant land snails once. They lived quite companionably in a glass tank on top of the washing machine. I used to think I had formed a bond with one of them, as he would seem to respond when I whistled for him, and he would slide towards me expectantly. But really, who was I kidding? Turns out, snails don't have ears. They have, though, got an excellent sense of smell. I still like to think he recognised me, but it was probably just the lettuce in my hand.

One of our previous dogs, Rocky, was our constant companion for twenty years. Not a bad age for a dog, but then smaller dogs do have a good old innings. He was smallish and wiry, a Patterdale Terrier with a tough short-hair coat of black and tan markings. His dog-like traits were fierce loyalty, and a huge appetite. He would demolish every meal with unseemly haste. He ate with a primal urgency, as if he feared apes were about to descend from the trees and steal his dinner. But

it wasn't just regular dog food that went down his gullet in a trice, he saw anything as a potential meal. He was not fussy: grass, twigs and whole sticks were pretty standard fare, but he also had a penchant for soft furnishings, carpets, five-pound notes, clothes, small rocks, whole almonds, tennis balls or indeed any item at floor level.

When we got him a companion, Ruby, a Lakeland Terrier, his desire to devour took on another dimension: he would eat things out of spite just so Ruby wouldn't get them, even if he didn't like them. I dropped a piece of orange peel once, and quick as a flash, Rocky was on it, gobbling it down, and glancing at Ruby in a smug, 'Ha, too late, sucker!' kind of way. Once he'd realised it wasn't something tasty like, I don't know, ham or a bit of skirting board, his enthusiasm waned somewhat. His chewing slowed and his normal fresh face curdled to a grimace. His lips curled back from his chops, his tongue began working overtime as the citrus bitterness produced inordinate amounts of saliva. As he chewed and dribbled, his eyes watered a little, and he looked miserable, but defiant. Ruby just watched impassively, perhaps with pity and amusement, and as he finally swallowed the last piece, he shuddered a little with relief, then strutted around in triumph.

On more than one occasion his eating habits required medical attention. I took him to our local vet.

'There seems to be an obstruction.'

'Could he have eaten something he shouldn't?'

You have no idea.

'Er, possibly.'

'He's panting a lot, I'll take his temperature.'

At this point, Rocky gave me an imploring look. The vet attempted to insert the thermometer into his rear end, but found it tricky.

'Mmm, there's something blocking here.'

And with admirable aplomb, the vet inserted a gloved finger.

As it went in, Rocky adopted a faraway, wistful expression as if he was remembering a *Radio Times* he'd eaten in 1989. The vet began pulling on whatever was causing the blockage. He gave a small tug, and the end of some orange plastic material appeared, so he began pulling. And pulling. It was like one of the worst magic tricks ever. As more of the evidence emerged, it became clear this was a shopping bag, on which was clearly printed the letter S. He pulled a bit more, a letter A appeared, then an I, an N . . . Time appeared to stand still as the word SAINSBURY'S gradually appeared from Rocky's rear end, who at this point gave a small bark, that I'm sure meant 'Ta-dah!'.

Two thoughts pinged into my brain. This would be a great way to teach kids how to spell. Get the dog to swallow various words on coloured ribbons, and then just wait. 'What's Rocky got for us this week?' And secondly, I can't see this making its way into a Sainsbury's ad any time soon.

There's evidence that shows our Neolithic ancestors thought highly of their dog companions. Dog skulls and bones were found buried alongside human remains dating back around four thousand years.

These dogs would have been the descendants of wolves, who would hang around the fringe of a human settlement for scraps. The boldest were adopted, and their offspring would have grown up alongside humans, and a long and beautiful friendship began.

There's something about their steadfast adoration that gives us joy. I know people who have been avowed non-dog people, then some scrawny mutt somehow wins them over. We can't help ourselves because they've wormed their way into our affection for thousands of years.

In an exhibition of whaling photographs, I was much taken with a shot of a beautiful engraving on a whale's tooth. It's an example of early scrimshaw attributed to the peoples of the north. It's a bit indistinct, but if you look closely you can clearly make out an Inuit elder pulling a fur bag from a husky's arse.

CONFRONTING YOUR FEARS (PART 2)

22

Weightless, suspended in a blue world, the clear sensations of up and down become blurred. The only sound I hear is my own breathing as I take short, mechanical sips of pressurised air which are then exhaled with a long and comically loud 'blub-blub-blub'. These are the surreal and beautiful sensations of scuba diving.

There is nothing quite like it. No comparable experience is available to us – well, not unless we are lucky enough to be astronauts. For me, it's not just the wonders of the undersea that are the thrill, but the chance to collect my thoughts, to focus on a physical activity that requires some concentration, a little dexterity and effort, and this focus turns the whole enterprise into a form of quiet contemplation. Because unless you've got some fancy headset kit, there's no talking to each

other underwater, so slow, deliberate hand movements are your only form of communication. As the cloud of blue surgeonfish flick and shimmer over the reef, time becomes elastic. I've been on dives that have felt like a brief dip in the water, and yet the dive watch tells of a fifty-minute submersion.

My breathing slows, as does my heart rate. The act of slow deep breathing, combined with the silence and weightlessness, is for me the nearest I get to meditation. And there are numerous other health benefits. Just the act of diving is good for the circulation and it can reduce blood pressure.

Aside from the obvious beauty of the undersea world, the physical otherness of diving comes a close second, personally. Being under the water is a constant source of wonder and delight, but it's also a major personal victory. A triumph of mind over matter.

Because the main reason I took up scuba diving was to conquer my fear of water.

On a school trip in Austria, I attempted to swim across a lake. I've since tried to track down the exact location. I'd like to think it was Lake Wolfgang just for the name alone, but it was more likely to have been the Zeller See, which is a beautiful spot, and great for swimming. No matter. I remember that it was a warm late summer's day and the calm surface of the lake framed by green alpine valleys was picture perfect. The water was a little cold, but it was not far across the lake and at the time I was a keen swimmer.

Yet halfway across, I suddenly felt a tightness in my chest, and a rising panic, which I realised afterwards was an asthma attack. I'd suffered from asthma as a child, and at one stage was using inhalers, but it had receded in my late teens and I had assumed, wrongly as it turned out, that it had gone away.

The surprise and severity of its return blindsided me, and as I flailed around, unable to breathe, the thought occurred to me that I might drown. Luckily there were plenty of folk around to haul me out, but it gave me a scare. For years after, I was nervous of the water, but the opportunity to dive in the tropics was too great a chance to pass up.

After seeing rays, octopus, shark, myriad species of fish and coral, the fear was gone, eclipsed by the submerged beauty. Asthma is sometimes stress-triggered. My reasoning went thus: 'If I can go under the water and not panic, it might help control my breathing.' In fact, many years and countless dives later, I can confirm this is exactly what it does.

Sometimes, there other reasons to get nervous underwater. On a trip around the World Heritage Site of Wayag in Eastern Indonesia, I dived with blacktip reef sharks. These puckish scroungers are not really dangerous – in fact, the guidebooks say they are only a threat 'if they feel cornered'. I spent much of the dive wondering if you can feel cornered in the ocean. Anyway, they were every bit as sleek and dynamic and amazing to watch under the water as I'd hoped, until I flipped up some sand and shells with my trailing fin, and in an instant all seven sharks turned in unison to face me and swam directly towards me.

Even though they're not particularly dangerous, it made me jump. I backed away, straight into an upright piling of a jetty and the jolt to the back made my pulse rate quicken. Sitting on the dive boat laughing about it later, I realised I had felt . . . cornered.

I know that diving might not be for everyone. There's no doubt you have to be fairly fit and in reasonably good health to even attempt it. All the lugging the gear around, the clumping about in tank and wetsuit is tiring. Not to mention the strain that being at depth puts on the body.

But I have included it in this book because, yes, it's a fun sport, a thing to do on your holidays, but it's more than that: it makes us have a greater appreciation for our world. It gives us a sense of place, or our impact on the planet, and on those creatures we share it with.

When I was diving in the crystal-clear winter swell of the Great Barrier Reef once, I looked into the eye of a minke whale and I defy anyone not to be struck with wonderment. I am changed forever, just as I was when I saw orangutans in the wild in Sumatra. When confronted with a creature so huge and sleek, benign and mysterious, so perfectly evolved, so at one with its environment, you find a resolve to try to do what you can for these creatures.

I've met many divers over the years, and I find a common thread among them. You'll find they all have a deep reverence for marine life, and a sense of purpose to do all they can to preserve and protect it. Diving soon becomes not just a pastime, but also an opportunity to look at the world in a different way.

Diving has also been a personal triumph for me. Being asthmatic, I was always told, well, that's not for you. And after my experience in

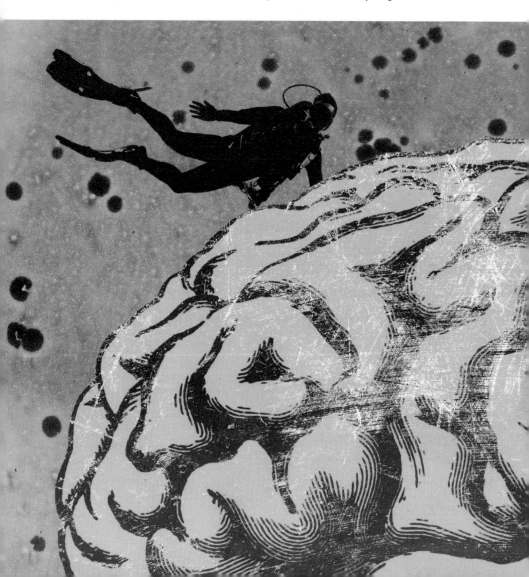

the Austrian lake, I had been wary of being immersed in water for years. Last year, I completed my Advanced Diver training and went wild swimming in a glacial fissure in Iceland, as you know. Diving for me is an example of how once you've identified your fears, they can be confronted, de-fanged and converted into happiness.

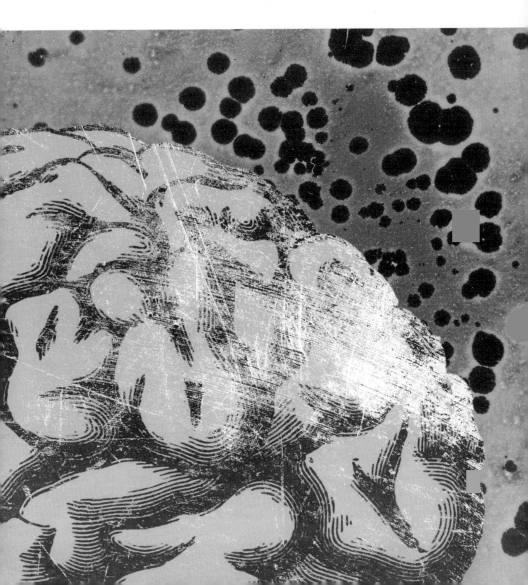

BIRDSONG

23

Over the course of a week in summer, I walked the Ridgeway, Britain's oldest road. After I'd been walking outdoors for several days, I realised my senses were getting keener. I could feel changes in the weather, air pressure and temperature. It was uncanny, but also reassuring how we are able to revert to a less desensitised version of ourselves. Our animal senses are always there, it's just that they are not called on that often. I was seeing more, hearing more, and in particular identifying birdsong: the distinctive intermittent drilling of a woodpecker, the insistent trilling of a yellowhammer, the raucous clamour of an alarmed pheasant, the surprisingly loud chattering of the wren, the mellifluous quivering of the blackbird . . .

According to research by The Sound Agency, birdsong can help us to focus, improve cognition and reduce tiredness. It also masks background noise that can be distracting. It can initiate a state in us that corresponds to 'body relaxed, mind alert'. To me, it's no wonder we feel calm when we hear birdsong, because over thousands of years, we've learned that when birds are singing, we're safe. It's when they stop singing that we need to worry.

One of the features that makes birdsong so relaxing is that it is stochastic, a word derived from ancient Greek meaning 'pertaining to chance'. In this context, it means that individual birds have a certain song, it's true, but it's not always predictable. The bird's song often changes slightly each time – a longer trill here, an embellishment there; plus, the recurrence is also random. This has a positive effect on us, in a way that a repetitive beat from a radio, or a drill, or anything non-organic might, well, drive us up the wall.

I remember waiting for a flight in Amsterdam's Schiphol airport and being struck by a strange feeling of freshness, of lightness of spirit. It wasn't the excellent slender triangle of Gouda I'd just eaten with an olive chaser, or the glass of chilled Pinot Grigio, although that couldn't have hurt. There was something else, almost indefinable. Then I realised – it was birdsong. I spend a lot of time in airports, and when I'm not trying to get on to the Wi-Fi, or just looking around for cheese, I spend my time watching people. There's something quietly comforting about recognising familiar types among your fellow humans, and Schiphol's airport was no exception: the grey-faced travellers, dazed and pallid after just having got off a long-haul flight; the short-haul moochers, hovering about the coffee bars, texting and laughing; the grey-suited business people hurrying to or from a flight, talking formally into their bluetooth earpieces; the families about to head out on holiday, all fired up and already dressed for the sunny destination in shorts and Hawaiian shirts, incongruous on this cold, drizzling January in the Netherlands.

And throughout all this there was this familiar throng, the unmistakeable sound of twittering birds, a mix of starlings, robins, blackbirds. But where from? I mean, I have seen actual living birds in airports, the odd sparrow that's flown in by mistake, or the occasional bemused pigeon, but the sound was coming from lots of birds. My eyes roved around in the mass of wire gantries suspending the array of signs, and then I spotted them. There were speakers mounted in living trees planted around the concourse. And from these emanated this avian chorus I could hear.

This creative initiative seems to have had an impact on travellers. Last time I looked, Amsterdam Schiphol has had over eleven thousand five-star Google reviews that extol its virtues of 'freshness', its 'friendliness', and how 'relaxing' it was. Perhaps they didn't even notice the birdsong, who knows? But its calming environment has not gone unnoticed in the airport world. A few years ago, Amsterdam was voted third best airport in the world at the World Airport Awards, to which my immediate response is, well done, well deserved and why wasn't I invited to host the World Airport Awards?

At the time of writing this, I'm at home with the back door to the garden ajar, the sounds of birds flooding through. It's a familiar chorus of our loudest and most enthusiastic singers: the soft fluting of a blackbird provides the backing vocals for the lead singer of a great tit, while the implausibly loud wren dukes it out with the nightclub MC shtick of a chaffinch. The usual sonic collage of traffic, planes overhead, radios and general city noise is absent, wonderfully so.

DANCING

24

Sometimes you just need to cut loose, cut a rug, let yourself go a little, and whether it's throwing shapes at the wedding/club/campsite, or just having a quiet boogie on your own, dancing is an excellent way of doing that. 'Alexa, play "Get Up Offa that Thing".'

Just for the avoidance of doubt, I am no lord of the dance, not even baronet of the dance, more caretaker of the dance. My signature move is a kind of elegant side-shuffle, a manoeuvre as deft as it is ancient, a shimmy such as a crab might make as it rears up on its hind legs. This is enhanced by flailing alternate arms and, on occasion, legs. It's rooted in modern jazz, tap and contemporary Klingon. I have just named it the Tango Nebula. Whether it follows any sort of pattern I have no idea, but I always feel better after I've executed it.

My most recent outing as a dance floor maven was at a birthday party in a little town in the south of France, where we ate *en plein air* in a courtyard restaurant. After dinner, the tables were cleared and moved back to make space for the dancing. The familiarity of the music and the company of friends uncorked a rare vintage of a night where songs were sung with full-throated intensity and lyrics were interpreted with a literal precision not seen since the days of Pan's People. The Nebula was given a full workout on the dance floor. Well, in this case, not so much a floor, more a kind of fine white gravel popular in France for the game of *boules*. In fact, I would say with hindsight that this space should have been exclusively used for boules. I wouldn't be surprised if, after that evening, the *patron* had put up a sign, prominently displayed with a stern warning: *Interdit de Danser! Seulement pour les Boules.* Instead the gravel-kicking, arm-flailing hoedown morphed into an inevitable and ill-advised conga line, with much cheering and whistling as the reluctant *patron* was coerced into the fray.

By the end of the night, my shirt, trousers and blue suede shoes were coated in that fine white powder, a flashback to Elvis's later years. They resembled prop shoes used in a film drama where the protagonist has been kidnapped in city clothes, kept hostage in a remote shack out in the desert, but has then somehow escaped and is now being pursued down a rocky gulch, and, acting his socks off throughout a hellish montage of dry riverbed/sun beating down/ circling vultures, has finally stumbled into a flyblown town near the Mexican border, his face all cracked lips and sunburn, croaking, 'Agua, agua.' Exactly like that.

I came second in a limbo-dancing competition once. Yes, I know you're sceptical, but it's true. It was during a charity fundraiser for a children's hospital, and I was a bit younger then and more bendy, but still. Each round saw the field whittled down as various denizens of the great and good fell away, until it was only me, Lionel Blair and Sinitta. After a close call I just scraped under the bar. Next up was Sinitta, but she tipped the bar off at the last second, so it was down to me and Lionel. His superior technique, honed by years of tap-dancing and charades eventually prevailed, and he took the honours, but I ran him very close.

As you know by now, I like finding out about the mental and physical benefits of my chosen routes to happiness. There are the obvious health benefits to The Dance, like improved heart and lungs, increased muscular strength, endurance and motor fitness, and increased aerobic fitness, if you're into that. Not to mention greater attractiveness to others, less embarrassment at family gatherings and generally a greater awareness of your place in the universe. OK, I started to make them up there, but you get the gist. It's an ancient thing, dance, it bonds us together, it lets us forget our daily troubles for a short while.

When I was a teenager, I had ballroom dancing lessons. There was a dance school across the road from our house and I learned the waltz, the foxtrot and the quickstep. The teacher was a tiny, petite woman with a huge passion for The Dance. It was a marvellous and quite surreal experience to whirl around a dance hall with this ball of terpsichorean energy. Bless her and all those she must have enlightened to her world. I can see the appeal of the foxtrot, the tango and the rhumba, the formal nature of it all, the practised moves, the precision, but it's not really me. I am more of a free-form mischief dancer, a Loki of the Lindy Hop.

I remember one night in Madrid, it was just the three of us – me, the wife and the teenage son – pogo-ing, headbanging and generally arsing about at a Foo Fighters concert. It remains one of my most cherished memories.

It's the best fun to dance like no one's looking among a crowd full of people.

PLEASURE

25

In 1873, the British philosopher John Stuart Mill wrote in his autobiography:

'Those only are happy . . . who have their minds fixed on some object other than their own happiness; on the happiness of others, on the improvement of mankind, even on some art or pursuit, followed not as a means, but as itself an ideal end. Aiming thus at something else, they find happiness by the way.'

I agree with the eminent Mr Mill here and his wisdom chimes with my own experience in that happiness is a fortunate by-product of purpose, generosity of spirit and a degree of luck. I have to say that I'm quite impressed that Mr Mill was able to have such a great handle on happiness, despite the austere nature of his upbringing. He was taught Greek from the age of three, and by the age of eight he had read *Aesop's Fables* and was acquainted with the dialogues of Plato. He was kept away from other children, lest their company sully the purity of his thought and distract him from the nobility of study. I can think of a lot of ways to describe his childhood and fun isn't one of them.

According to his autobiography, he went through a period of great sadness as he left his teenage years behind, as he considered what would make him happy. His life's ambition was to create a just society, a noble and selfless one no doubt, but when he asked himself the question, 'Would this make me happy?' the answer was, 'No'. Luckily,

he was brought out of his melancholy by the poetry of Wordsworth, which reminded him of joy and beauty, both of which were perhaps a little lacking in his formative years.

I think he was asking himself the wrong question. If it had been, 'John, do you reckon that a stroll in the woods, a round of dinosaur golf, then a pint in the Seven Bells would make you happy?' I'll bet the answer would have been, 'Yes'. It might not have led to a lifetime dedicated to the improvement of mankind, or to him becoming the most influential English-speaking philosopher of the nineteenth century, but it might have cheered him up a bit.

In my dealings with happiness, I find it helps to be easily pleased. I am a simple soul for whom simple pleasures bring ample rewards. Removing the peel from a satsuma in one piece, making the perfect cup of tea and finding one last oatcake in the packet will elicit from me a clenched fist pump of victory.

And yes, of course I feel a profound happiness at having been fortunate enough to experience love, and thus finding a sense of belonging, of knowing my place in the wider scheme of things. This is the deeper flow of happiness, but I can be made equally happy by a well-made toasted sarnie.

When I was fifteen, my mother expressed concern that I wanted to go out with my friends again. She said, 'Life is not always about pleasure.' As a teenager, the idea of life not being about pleasure seemed ludicrous. Life is pleasure, isn't it? It's all there is! Pleasure all the way!

Today, though, her words resonate with me more. If by pleasure you mean hedonism, larks, fun, then yes, it is just one aspect of happiness, and its appeal changes over time. The idea that there can be different kinds of happiness is an old one, argued over by the Greek philosophers. If I could go back to that mother and son conversation, and briefly inhabit my teenage self, I might have said, 'Well, Mum, I can see you're veering more towards Aristotle's view of happiness, that requires adherence not just to an ethical lifestyle, but a degree of virtue, whereas I myself am leaning more towards Epicurus in his pursuit of pleasure as a means of happiness. Unlike the Aristotlean view, shared by the Stoics, the Cynics and to some extent the Sceptics, the Epicurean philosophy identifies happiness not with virtue, but with pleasure. Which I think is equally valid so in some ways we're both right.'

But at the time, I just said, 'I'm going to see the Stranglers.'

And later that evening I stood in the crowd in Bath Pavilion and watched the Stranglers play in all their glorious pomp. I sang lustily along to 'Hanging Around', 'Duchess' and stood agog at the drumming on 'Genetix'. At one point, Jean-Jacques Burnel took off his bass guitar and started hurling it around his head, which was unbelievably exciting. John Stuart Mill would have admired the beauty of that moment.

On my way home the electric thrill of it sparked and crackled through my limbs. Joy unbridled! A night filled with pleasure of which Epicurus himself would have approved.

JOGGING

26

Running is an evolutionary hangover from chasing prey all day. A stop-start affair where, as the pursuer, you should be prepared to be in it for the long haul. To be honest, if I'd been chasing a deer all day, and finally caught up with it, I probably wouldn't have the strength to then wrestle it to the ground. I can imagine one of my Neanderthal ancestors slumped, wheezing against a rock, imploring the deer to give itself up, and just hurl itself into a pot out of sympathy. The deer looks on in pity, then effortlessly skips away, as the knackered would-be hunter eats a clump of moss and vows to become the first Neanderthal vegan.

As a part-time, half-hearted fair-weather jogger, I think I have identified two types of runner. Type As are as lean and wiry as champion whippets with zero per cent body fat, an effortless loping gait and faces as smooth and calm as terracotta warriors. Type Bs weigh about three stone more than Type As, are red and puffy of face, and wear a pained, desperate expression bordering on terror. They look like people whose corporate crimes have caught up with them, and to avoid capture, they are having to run away, possibly for the first time in their lives.

It is my life's ambition to switch from Type B to Type A.

Running is hugely popular, and as a way to get fit, hard to beat. It's simple and doesn't require too much specialised kit – you just need some decent shoes, some kind of breathable fabric T-shirt, shorts and a bra, and you're off.

Having said that, it's hard not to be impressed by the rumbling juggernaut that is the running industry. In 2017, the global running shoe market was valued at $64 billion. That's just the shoes, never mind all the fancy clothing, the health drinks, the gadgets. The headband market alone is worth $23 billion (I imagine).

I have tried an assortment of running apps, although I'm not entirely sure they're aimed at the Type B stumbler. All I want from them is hard data, distance, running time, and maybe some calorie-burning information, not the clubby, slightly smug atmosphere that assumes that you can't wait to 'connect' with the 'running community' and share your runs with your new 'friends'. There's no way I'm doing that. 'Hey guys, here's "Bill in Hammersmith" (no profile photo). He's

Jogger Type 'A'

Jogger Type 'B'

run 5km in a time that someone on crutches could probably improve on.' Yeah, can't wait to share that with my new 'friends'. A quick glance at these posts and you get an idea of the prancing, bronzed showponies that you're dealing with. They are all ludicrously fit ultrathon Iron Man/Woman Tough Mudders who have 'just popped out for a seventeen-miler' which was 'super great'. Here's a photo of me in some tight lycra in some implausibly beautiful part of Arizona or whatnot. Not bent double wheezing like a rusty accordion in a Tesco car park.

No, I will not be sharing, but that's fine. The thing is, I actually like running. I understand its popularity, and I can see the benefits. I like the simplicity of it. Don't overthink it, Bill! But I did. I tried one of those armband mobile phone holders. After fiddling around trying to get the app started, I then inserted the phone into the sleeve, and Velcro'd it to my upper arm. I'd managed only to get about a hundred yards from my house when the whole thing started to slide down onto my elbow, then onto my forearm.

If this happens to you, never try to wrestle it back up while running. I nearly took out a bollard, ran into a post box, and wobbled out into traffic. So I had to stop, reposition and cinch the Velcro a little tighter. *Oh great*, I thought, *there goes my time. Won't be able to share that with the community.* As I cruised past Primark, it seemed to be holding.

After the turnaround at 2.5k, I meandered a little by the river. If this was a 5k race, I am sure that stopping for the view would probably be frowned on. I leaned on the river wall, grateful for the heat from the sun-warmed stone on my numbed hands, and watched the sunlight glint off the flood tide as some fuzzy Canada goslings paddled after their mum.

At this point, I felt suddenly dizzy; my head swam as I rocked back and forth, gripping the wall for support. I traced the feeling of discomfort to my arm, to where the phone holder gripped my bicep like an Illuminati's *cilice* belt. In order to secure it in place, I'd done it up too tight, and now it resembled the device the doctors use to check your blood pressure. Undoing the strap released a dam-busting flow of blood through my arm that drained away from my vitals with such force that I nearly fainted into a hedge. After steadying myself on the wall again, I set off once more.

This time, I tried running with the phone holder a bit looser, but it ended up around my wrist, so I just took the whole thing off, put it in my pocket and ran holding the phone in front of me. I persevered with this device but maybe my arms are the wrong shape, or I'm not adhesive enough. It either feels like something I'd wear for an elbow strain or like that sensation you get when you're handling a boa constrictor at a reptile encounter and something has spooked it.

So now I run, free of pressure, not sharing my times or routes, incognito in my baseball hat, holding my phone in one hand. I still get the running high; I enjoy the sensations of being out on the streets, of knowing the potholes to avoid in the road, tripping lightly around the unevenness of the pavement like a mature gazelle. What I lack in speed I now make up for with agility. Each time, the wheezing is a little less, the post-run high a little greater.

On my route, I pass three other blokes of a similar vintage to me, all clutching a phone in their hands. We share a knowing smile, raise our phones in a toast, and jog on.

CYCLING

27

I'm poised atop a ridge on a mountain bike trail deep in a pine forest, inhaling lungfuls of the scented air. My heart is pumping and my legs are complaining from the steep climb. I am grateful for the full suspension and hydraulic brakes on this missile of a bike; plus, I will never tire of the remote saddle dropper button on the handlebars. As I push off, I glimpse a deer crossing the path ahead. Ah, to be at one with nature. The sensation of speed, of freedom. This is what cycling is about! As I rattle down the trail, I let out an involuntary whoop.

Much as I love cycling, I rarely whoop involuntarily on a bike in central London. I have, instead, waited at traffic lights amidst a scowling peloton of angry lycra, and tried smiling and mumbling pleasantries, only to be met with silence and looks of incomprehension and often pity. There's not much camaraderie, just testosterone-fuelled competitiveness, coupled with a strong survival instinct, which I

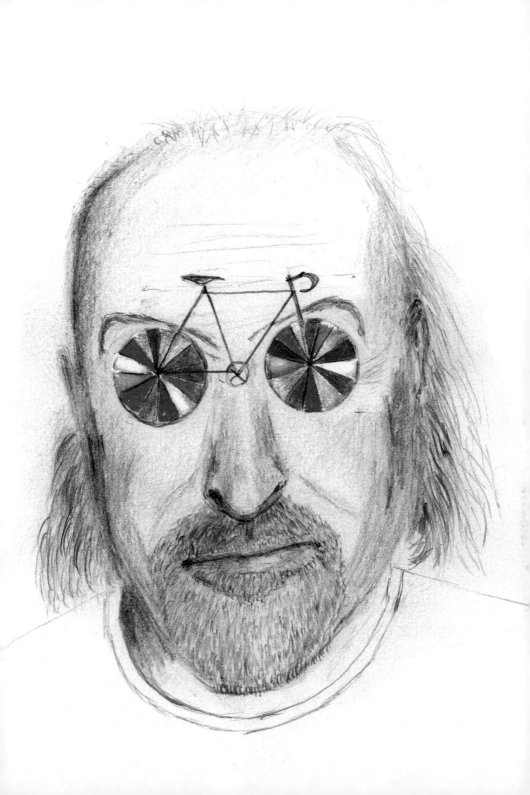

suppose is essential in a city like London. I was once smeared down the side of a black cab at Hyde Park Corner. My hands and startled face became pliant in contact with the window glass, causing great alarm to the commuters within. 'Wasn't that whatsisname?' 'Couldn't tell. His face was too squishy.'

Compare this to the friendlier biking of Amsterdam, where no one wears a helmet. No hi-vis, no special gear, just people whose faces are visible, barrelling along on old-fashioned bikes, half smiling as they trrrring their bells and look happy in a practical Dutch way.

According to British Cycling, the sport's governing body in the UK, more than two million people cycle at least once a week these days during lockdown. There have never been this many people cycling in Britain. Sales of bikes are at an all-time high. Tabloid headlines reflect a general tizzy about the whole thing. 'Stop this cycle lane madness!' they say. 'Cycle Lanes – how they may affect HOUSE PRICES!'

This renaissance in British cycling is a remarkable turnaround since the 1960s when sales of bikes were actually falling. City planners back then were not keen on factoring in cycle lanes, which has led to this awkward retrofitting which we see now. I never feel entirely safe on a road between some painted lines saying 'cycle lane', much as I wouldn't feel entirely safe swimming between floating markers in Cape Cod that said 'shark-free lane'.

Compare this to the more enlightened planners of Denmark and Holland who have never fallen out of love with bikes. In Copenhagen, there are dedicated, raised cycle lanes through the city. In the Netherlands, on my recent tour there, a heavily tattooed and multiple-pierced roadie told me, 'We grew up on bikes.' And to look at him, you'd think he meant Harleys, not 1950s midwife bikes with green plastic muffin crates bungee-strapped to the handlebars.

One of the few times I've enjoyed city cycling is on New Year's Eve when a large part of central London was closed to traffic. I was performing in town, and it was the best way to get home. It was a delight to cycle through London under the Christmas lights in roads free of traffic. The only accompaniment was the sound of footfall and the buzz of excited conversation: a glimpse of what a city centre could be without motors, and all the better for gliding through it on two wheels. Weaving my way through the happy revellers, cycling up Regent Street on the wrong side of the road, I laughed, and whooped involuntarily.

BEING SOMEONE TO RELY ON

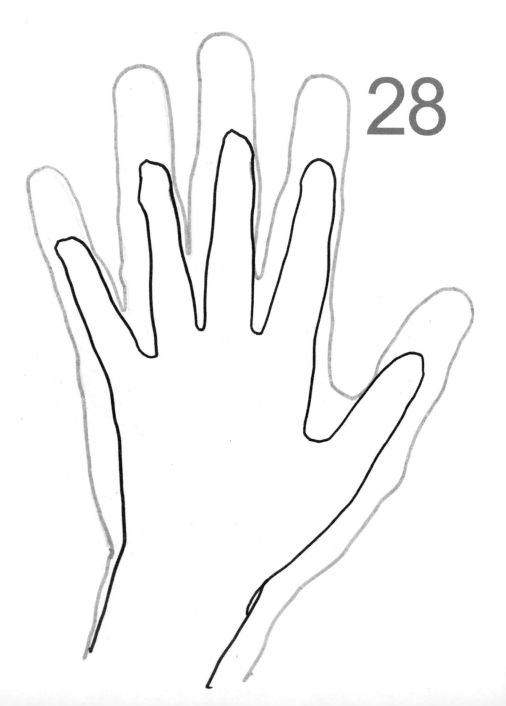

28

According to the UN's 'World Happiness Report', Finland has been declared the world's happiest country three years in a row. But Finland excels in ways that might not appear immediately happy-inducing.

Some of you are now thinking, *I know you like Finland, Bill, but really? If you're looking for a country that exudes happiness, one that positively thrums with felicitous vibes, then surely there's a whole continent of them in South America that you'd pick before Finland, no?*

It would have to be some sun-kissed Latin idyll where laughing, shiny people spontaneously shimmy around some handbags outside a post office in Cartagena to the strain of a busking vallenata ensemble, or dance to the soft sounds of samba floating seductively from a boombox artfully placed by some casual sun-worshippers on the Copacabana Beach in Rio. Or if dancing isn't your thing, the tongue-tasering, mood-elevating zing of ceviche from the world's greatest street food in Lima, surely that's the continent for happiness, Bill! Not the freezing, lake-pitted Winterfell of austere Finland, where it's dark for eleven months of the year, or something.

And the Finns, aren't they all called Aki or Anti and are dour and introspective, and mope about Helsinki sighing, or drinking, or a combination of both while lugubrious, impenetrable Finnish music plays in brutalist, Soviet-era workers' canteens as the benighted Finns mechanically fork some boiled cabbage into their mournful mouths?

Yes, well it is a bit like that. And there's an element of truth in both.

The UN 'World Happiness Report' has six main criteria on which it judges its findings, and some of them are what you might expect. The GDP per capita, life expectancy, freedom to make life choices, and freedom from corruption. All very laudable, and evidence of good governance and a balanced and healthy society. Finland has all of these attributes, but there are a couple of less obvious ones that are worth delving into, because these are more about getting under the skin of a place, perhaps even divining the soul of a country. One is generosity, which I will deal with a little later in this book, and the other is almost shocking in its simplicity.

Having someone you can count on.

The stark simplicity of that took me by surprise. This is why I really rate these reports, because they don't just collate bland facts and figures, or count the cost of living in euros or krøne. They aren't about how much money you have, or whether there's adequate parking in the town centre, or whether the footpaths are well maintained. Of course, these are all important but the real nub of this report gets to the heart of what happiness is. To me this means how is your daily existence? Do you feel content, secure? Can you rely on someone?

If anything positive can come from this strange and surreal self-isolation, it is that we should be more neighbourly. Away from our video calling and remote communication, our physical worlds have shrunk down to a few households in the immediate vicinity, and the people in our neighbourhood feel more like family. We have run a few errands and done some shopping for our neighbours, and likewise others have helped us out in all kinds of ways. It seems only right that it is on these small acts that a country's happiness index can be gauged.

But I think reliance goes beyond what is in the UN's report. It specifies that having someone to rely on elicits happiness. I would say that's true; it gives you a sense of relief, and a reassurance that someone has your back. But I would suggest from my own experience that it works both ways. Being relied on, having that responsibility and knowing that there is a reciprocal sense of community in this scary time feels like a strength, resilience that I hope will endure long after these strange lockdown days are over.

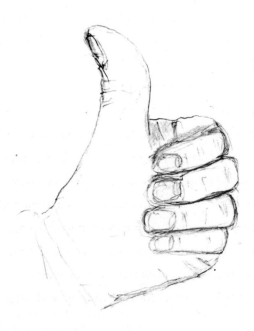

WALKING

29

A brisk walk is a great pick-me-up, but if you're intent on something a bit more than a stroll to the park, take the advice of Thomas Jefferson, who said, 'Walking is the best possible exercise. Habituate yourself to walk very far.'

Which is what I am doing right now.

I am reclining on a soft turf bank in England. It's late morning in the summertime. Squinting upwards, I follow the progress of a skylark into the holly blue, silver-washed sky. I've slipped off my walking shoes and socks to rub my feet a little, letting them luxuriate in the cool grass. The high ridge of our location affords a stunning view over the Chiltern Hills on one side, and the Thames Valley on the other.

As if this moment could not be bettered, I'm handed a piece of homemade layer cake to accompany the camping mug of tea cooling at my side. Bliss.

I am walking the oldest road in Europe, the Ridgeway, which is about ninety miles of mostly remote path that connects some of the oldest and most Outstandingly Natural Beautiful Areas of old England.

Around me are friends and family who've joined this long-distance endeavour. The plan is to walk the length of the Way, plus a little bit extra at the start where it joins with the Icknield Way, to get it up to one hundred miles and raise some money for charity in the process. We have been staying in B & Bs and pubs, and after fifteen odd miles of walking each day, beds have never felt softer, breakfasts have never tasted so delicious, cups of tea have never been so relished.

Walking is the simplest and perhaps most underrated of outdoor activities. I like all kinds of walking, from jungle treks to nipping to the shops for teabags. Whatever the reward is, a view or a pint, or just a cup of tea and a lie-down, walking can be an endless source of happiness. Provided I have the correct footwear. Among those things that really get my goat, like incorrect spelling or rudeness, having the wrong type of shoe for a required activity is right up there.

For me, the thrill isn't so much walking for walking's sake. I like the thrill of a walking challenge, especially when there is wildlife along the way that can elevate the experience. One such occasion was a coast-to-coast hike I took across the island of Seram, in Eastern Indonesia, the aim being to see some of the island's unique bird species.

From Wahai on Seram's rugged northern coast, a group of us hiked for two weeks through dense tropical rainforest in the wet season. Our progress was slow, as the path was not well trodden so the mud sucked and clawed at our boots as we threaded our way through ancient jungle, while biting insects and leeches came along for the ride. There aren't many cafés in Seram's dense interior, so our daily sustenance consisted of dried fish, rice and noodles.

But these hardships are quickly forgotten when you are dazzled by a livid green Eclectus parrot, or stopped in your tracks by the pterodactyl-esque wing-whoosh of a Blyth's hornbill, and then, resting on a fallen tree trunk for a moment, find renewed appreciation for a satsuma.

At the end of each day, other treats lay in store for us that made the privations worthwhile. Overseas visitors are a rarity for the remote villages in the interior, so our arrival was always a huge novelty. The sight of a bunch of rain-sodden, mud-spattered, wild-eyed loons stumbling out of the jungle was for the village kids tremendous entertainment. The more they laughed and pointed, the more we played up to it, clowned around, pulled faces and silly-walked like idiots.

Sometimes the end-of-walk reward takes on a less gratifying, unexpected form. On a walking holiday in northern Spain, our plan was to take the path from Bigues i Riells up the valley to the

Fig. 9 - *Correct footwear = happiness*

spectacular eleventh-century Sant Miquel del Fai, a Benedictine monastery perched on a rocky outcrop that juts out from a vertiginous cliff face. It was hard going under the Catalan sun that beat down on us as we toiled up the rocky trail, threading our way through the orchards and olive groves. Again, this effort was rewarded by birdlife, this time with glimpses of dazzling European bee-eaters, richly coloured and rarely seen in Britain but common in these latitudes.

At the summit of this path, we paused to take in the view. We looked down across valleys of olives and little villages, with the mountains receding into the afternoon haze. We sat by a waterfall in reverential silence, taking in the atmosphere of this place, and considered our return journey. To have trodden in the footsteps of monks whose path was still the only way to reach this sacred site felt humbling and somehow reassuring, like nothing had changed in a thousand years.

A member of staff who spoke perfect English asked if we had enjoyed our time. I said we had and that we were looking forward to the walk back down to our hotel.

'You can take a cab back if you like,' he said. 'Lot easier.'

'Really?'

'Yep, there's a cab rank round the back, you go up the stairs, past the gift shop, and it's just across the car park.'

Somehow the spell of this mysterious place was broken. To be honest, I was secretly relieved as it had been a long haul. So, after some ice creams and a few purchases from the gift shop that included a bag of marbles, some postcards, coasters bearing the faces of some notable Benedictine monks, a couple of mugs and a tea-towel, we were whisked back to our accommodation down the mountain.

The steep path up to the monastery had only really been wide enough for one person, so the chance for conversation and banter had been curtailed a little. In these situations, you tend to just put your head down, plant your feet down in a steady rhythm and become withdrawn into your own thoughts. Which I imagine had suited your average monk.

For more sociable walking, I must admit I favour the wide chalk downs and worn meadow-paths that characterise large sections of the Ridgeway, where you can happily stroll along and there is enough space to be easily flanked by other folk you can blether with away all day. There's something quite congenial about the side by side conversation, that is less intense than a direct face-to-face exchange. No eye contact need be made, your direction of travel is the same, you can just drop back out of the chat, or accelerate on, without the need for some awkward British apology.

Towards the end of the hundred-mile hike, conversations became notably more terse, along the lines of, 'How much further?' or 'Whose idea was this?' which for any non-British people translates as: 'I am having the best time, you are my fond companion.'

177

LETTER WRITING

30

I'm doing something ludicrously old-fashioned and archaic: I am writing a letter with a pen and paper. Watching the characters form as the pen flows across the page is more satisfying than seeing these words appear on my computer screen.

Handy though emails are, there is no substitute for the writing and receiving of handwritten letters.

It is an enduring provider of happiness. The act of writing engages your motor skills and your memory – helping to sharpen the mind. In a study conducted by the University of Washington, students who wrote their essays with pen and paper tended to write more and faster, and in more complete sentences than those who used keyboards.

And apparently the act of handwriting itself stimulates a part of the brain called the Reticular Activating System, or RAS. The RAS acts as a filter for all the stuff the brain is trying to process, helping you to concentrate, and one of the ways to trigger it is the physical act of writing. Writing letters is good for you!

Aside from these practical benefits, for me there's an intimacy about a letter, an emotional power. I love the feel of the paper, the crisply folded sheets. The imprint left by the writer, the telltale character of their unique handwriting, the odd slip of the pen. I once received a letter from a friend who liked to smoke, and when I opened the envelope, I inhaled the unmistakable aroma of her clove cigarettes. This exotic fragrance had attached itself to the paper, and as I read her words, her physical presence momentarily entered the room.

I have a collection of letters from my grandmother and my mother, who were both enthusiastic letter writers. These have become keepsakes, mementos. Letters can have great power, and lasting influence. I don't see anyone printing off emails and framing them anytime soon.

After I met the woman who I would later marry, we wrote to each other. I sent her some flowers. She wrote to thank me. I wrote back, and we continued our correspondence for a year, before she finally moved from Edinburgh and joined me in London. It was our courtship, if that's not a too comically antiquated term. And it was conducted via letters.

It won't come as any surprise, though, that writing by hand is on the decline. A recent survey confirms this. Of the two thousand people who took part, one in three hadn't written anything by hand in the previous six months. Nothing, not even a Post-it note. Because let's be honest, can we be bothered to write letters? Email is so much more convenient. Just the process of writing and posting this letter is a right palaver. Collecting the paper, the pens, the envelope, the stamp, walking to the post box . . . Blimey, in that time I could have written a dozen emails, ordered a multipack of hiking socks, booked a holiday, watched a YouTube clip of trawlers in high seas, renewed my parking permit and not once left my garden table.

In a mid-autumn festival in Nanjing University, staff suggested to the students that they handwrite a letter to their parents. It was the first time any of them had ever done such a thing. One mother wrote back to her daughter, saying the day she'd received her letter was the happiest of her life.

If that's still not enough of an incentive for you to write a letter, what about postcards? I have made it a ritual every time I am on tour, regardless of where I am, to send one. Friends and family are just as likely to receive a postcard of Swindon Town Centre 1968 as they are of Monument Valley, the pier at Weston-Super-Mare or the Northern Lights of Trømso.

So I urge you, make the effort. If a letter seems too onerous, a card will be fine. Just gather the writing paraphernalia. Order it online if you have to. Go through your address book, and put pen to paper. It will make someone happy.

Mainly you.

I wrote you a letter!
Wow! thanks!
Can you take a photo of it and text it to me?
hahaha
I'm serious
I've already sent it
how long will it take
2-3 working days
hahahaha lol
I'm serious
hello??

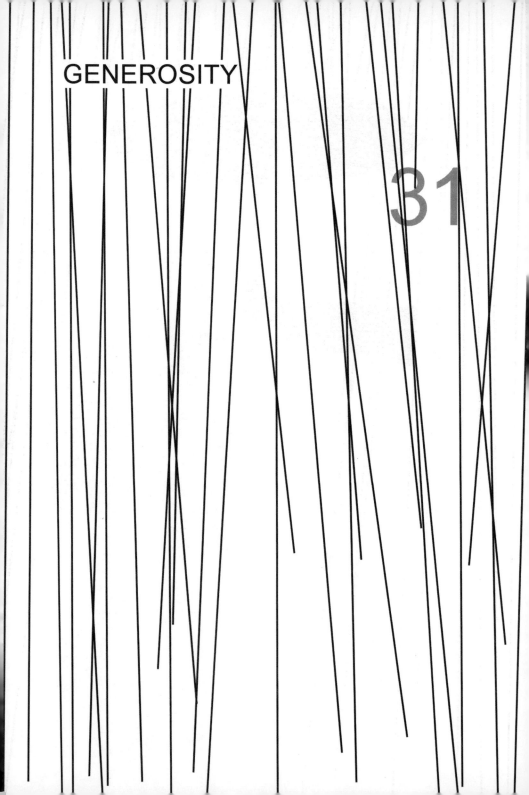

GENEROSITY

31

Britain gives more to charity per head of population than any other country in Europe. We may be a strange and contradictory bunch, prone to eccentricity, self-deprecation, awkwardness, deflection, arrogance, absurdity, humility and outbursts of nostalgia, but we are generally good people. Whatever the caveats that may exist about charity – making up government shortfall, where does the money go? etc. – it's still a heartening statistic. At the time of writing, a hundred-

year-old army veteran called Captain Tom Moore has raised nearly £33 million for the NHS by walking laps of his garden. These are tough and extraordinary times no doubt, so this is an incredible achievement.

Giving to those in need, acts of kindness and generally helping others out is not only a good thing, there can also be some net benefit to us in the form of our own well-being. And at this point, I detect that some of you may be sceptical. You may have given to others, and got nothing from it; you may have lent a cordless drill to a neighbour without so much as a custard cream in return. Various charitable direct debits might leave your bank account every month with no discernible flicker of joy on your happiness radar. You may well ask, 'Altruism. What's in it for me?'

Well, you'll be pleased to know that researchers from the University of Zurich have established a neural link between giving and happiness. Their 2017 study suggested that giving to others activates areas of the brain related to selflessness and the reward cycle, specifically our nexus of generosity, the temporo-parietal junction and the happiness zone, the ventral striatum. Activity at the temporo-parietal junction has been associated with altruism, generosity and overcoming egocentricity bias, which then in turn causes activity in the ventral striatum, part of the brain associated with reward and pleasure.

MRI scans of participants showed interactions between these brain regions when they performed a generous act. So basically, the brain is rewarding our lack of self-interest, our 'other-regarding' behaviour, with a good toot on the brain's happiness horn, so to speak. You could argue that down on the corner, at the junction of West Temporo and East Ventral, is the hot dog stand of Morality.

Another study showed that giving to others or just spending time with others can reduce stress, give you a sense of purpose, improve your mental health and blood pressure, and even increase your longevity. Where do I sign up?

The word 'generous' itself comes via old French from the Latin *generosus*, meaning 'of noble birth', a connotation which is now obsolete, although you could argue there is a certain nobility in the practice. Usage of the word 'generous' has somewhat depressingly been in gradual decline since its heyday in the late eighteenth century, which oddly saw a huge spike in 1779. That year coincided with the founding of various public dispensaries, so perhaps it was this which prompted such an outpouring of goodwill. If the treatments and cures of 1779 written by a certain Dr Mead were anything to go by, you were going to need plenty of goodwill. For fevers, he prescribed 'bleeding, drinks of London porter, powdered Peruvian bark, orange peel, gentle exercise and a mild nourishing diet', which almost exactly replicates a typical day at the Glastonbury Festival.

Once certain words have been brought together in a certain role, they find themselves typecast, unable to move on. I have never heard of an injunction that wasn't 'slapped', or a ring of steel that wasn't 'thrown'. 'Generous' has a bit more leeway, and gets used to describe not just people and gestures, but chairs, patios, hotel rooms, cupboards. Do your ventral striatum a favour and pop round your neighbours' with some chocolate brownies.

To me, it's simple: if you give to others, you benefit in ways you might not have foreseen. Being charitable with your time also has the valuable side effect of selflessness. Not in the sense of pious martyrdom, but simply in that it removes the focus from you and places it on someone else. On occasion we can become completely wrapped up in ourselves, and not necessarily via the usual pitfalls of vanity or self-importance. Sometimes we are just stuck, unable to function, entwined in our knotted thoughts. Like the tangled tails of adolescent squirrels, our worries are all pulling in different directions but going nowhere, a squirrel-king of competing qualms and trepidations.

Thinking about others can help throw some much-needed perspective on your own situation, and can perhaps even release *The Squirrels of Unease*, which I like to think was the unpublished prequel to *The Dogs of War*.

BELONGING

32

I'm headbanging at a Metallica concert, lost in the moment. A few seconds ago, they intro'd 'Enter Sandman' and the familiar diminished fifth chords send a pulse of pure rock energy through the assembled hordes. When the main riff growls into life, huge gouts of flame burst from the stage, a deafening roar erupts from the crowd, and I feel pumped with adrenaline, as if I were about to charge into battle against Saruman's Uruk-hai, or at the very least, fling myself down a steep hill after a wheel of cheese. My head nods back and forth more furiously than ever, my fingers twitch manically and in a few seconds I'm committed to a proper headbang and air-guitar combo.

After what seems an age of bone-shaking riffage, I pause for breath at the end of the song. I look around and catch the eye of another fan, who's also paused, knackered but elated, and we share a smile and raised rock horns. I take in the loving energy of the huge crowd beyond us and, closer to home, the golden glow that has lit up the faces of my gang around me, as if the treasure chest of life's secrets has been briefly revealed to us. All seems well with the world in that moment.

Of course, these little live-wire contact-buzzings with our fellow humans don't happen exclusively at metal concerts. I have found myself watching the sunrise over Avebury Stone Circle on the morning of the summer solstice, and high-fived a tie-dyed poncho-wearing compadre. I have been at the checkout of my local corner shop with

a bag of crisps and a bottle of wine and the person behind me had exactly the same crisps and wine, and he said, 'great minds', and it made me smile. Is this just our craving for a bit of connection in our fragmented brave new world, or something deeper?

A yearning perhaps, for the close bonds of society our ancestors enjoyed? Maybe we miss being in a nomadic tribe of hunter-gatherers. The headbanging, the solstice and the crisps and wine all have their corresponding versions of our ancient selves. We like to belong, that's the truth of it, because it makes us happy.

We're social animals, us humans. Maddeningly contradictory, often baffling and mildly eccentric, we nonetheless seek out others. We've always thrived in groups, and lived and worked in small communities. Only relatively recently have we started to live more solitary lives.

According to a study by Nottingham Trent University, the more an individual identifies with their family, friends, local community, religious group, band or sports team, the happier they are.

I have come to realise over the years that I've always been a little out of step with the mainstream of society. I am quite content with this, having long ago come to terms with it. Being bearded, long-haired and slightly odd looking, I have always identified with the outsider, and, pre-TV recognition, the slight unease my appearance would elicit from other people on a train. They would eye me warily as if I had a jug of homemade cider in a woven basket under my seat, or a dog on a string, or a praying mantis in a jar. To be fair, I have actually had all these things, so these were not unreasonable concerns.

In the ensuing years, the eyeing warily on the train usually preceded a selfie. But in society at large, not much has changed. It's as if I'm some kind of shield bug scuttling along in one direction, and I encounter a column of ants coming the opposite way who are all chatting away about some ant-based gossip I know nothing about. 'Yes, I know, I heard that from one of the sentinels. Oh, it's that shield bug - don't look, he's probably got an aphid on a string'.

My great luck in life, is having found something that I love doing, that supports me and the family, and has given me purpose and a tribe. Finding comedy and the company of other comics is like seeing other kinds of shield bug, all going the same way, and we see each other, we wave, and acknowledge that there's a bond between us. I never forget to thank my good fortune.

If you want to headbang to your favourite metal track, you can do this on your own, of course. No one can stop you! Go crazy! Once when I was alone in a hotel room I played air-guitar and leapt about like a dervish to all nine magnificent minutes of Blue Öyster Cult's live version of 'Don't Fear the Reaper'. During the middle eight I lost my balance and banged into the wardrobe, causing the door to fly open and an ironing board to fall out on top of me, but I felt no fear. It was a bit rock and roll, and I felt OK with it, because it's what Blue Öyster Cult would have wanted.

BEING IN NATURE

33

In the course of my reading on the subject of happiness, a word drifted across my transom: 'ecopsychology', the study of the mental health benefit of being in nature. The word is credited to a Theodore Roszak who first coined the term in 1992 in his book *The Voice of the Earth*. His main premise is that our minds are shaped by the modern world but originate in nature, and we have suffered as a result of this disconnect. Our diminishing engagement with nature is affecting our, well, happiness. His views echo those of the great biologist E. O. Wilson who said that humans have an instinct to emotionally connect with nature.

To all of which I say yes, and yes. We like to think of ourselves as sophisticated creatures, capable of understanding abstract concepts like morality, freedom and consciousness, even happiness. We can start sourdough and spiralise courgettes, while mastering Spanish and video calling. We talk in depth about TV shows and gadgets and politics, but underneath this veneer of twenty-first-century cool, we're animals after all, prone to atavistic desires to be outdoors and frolic like fauns in the forest or trip lightly up mountains like wheezing chamois; to do sideways rolls down a grassy bank or eat pasties up in the sand dunes like guilty raccoons.

But what is new is that policymakers, healthcare professionals and even governments are realising that the benefits of being in nature are not just something writers, ramblers and whiskery country folk have been banging on about for centuries, but a significant medical resource to be tapped for the health of the nation.

The signs have been arriving steadily. On a stand-up tour of Orkney and Shetland a few years ago, I was reminded anew what a beautiful place this was for walking outdoors and birdwatching, but also delighted to discover that these very activities were actually being prescribed by local doctors on the NHS, for a variety of medical conditions ranging from heart disease to diabetes, or depression and anxiety to high blood pressure.

'Two guillemots every four hours, and if symptoms persist, a long walk across the moor.'

Just knowing this makes me happy.

With a mum and dad both working in the NHS as nurse and doctor respectively, I was brought up to always trust in medicine, in clinical trials, in solid science. But I welcome this shift in attitude that embraces other forms of treatment that don't rely on just prescribing medication, but offer actual tangible, medical benefits from being outdoors, and following outdoor pursuits.

After cross-referencing thousands of volunteers and assessing their experience of being out in a green space, a study done by Exeter University has arrived at a definitive minimum amount of time spent in nature that yields tangible results: just two hours of outdoor time a week is enough to see a marked increase in the benefits of being in nature. And it doesn't even have to be in one go, as long as the cumulative outdoors time adds up to two hours. So, you could spend twenty minutes a day in your local park or save up and binge on a long walk at the weekend, the result is the same.

There has always been talk about a Green Deal, or a New Green Revolution, and we're living in a time of climate crisis, no doubt. As we emerge from this pandemic, will we just go back to normal? Live exactly as we were doing? The sceptical side of me says, yeah, probably. But we can hope that this enforced slow-down of civilisation has given a boost to all this progressive thinking. Not just to our immediate neighbours, but on a global scale. A little less consumption, a little more kindness. Perhaps a greater appreciation not just of the healing power of nature, but the hard-commercial gain of fewer meds, less hospitalisation, more natural treatment. Good health means a better bottom line.

And a note to new city planners: open spaces in cities are more important than ever for all of our mental well-being. Not just a place to sit on your phone looking at cat gifs, or to let your kids play, or read a book, or eat your lunch, or just stare into the sky in a daydream. We need a place where we can observe others, to see how others live. We're social animals, we're gregarious and curious, we thrive among others, we do better when we help each other and work together. Sometimes that's all it takes to be happy.

SPEAKING ANOTHER LANGUAGE

34

OK, so you can say, *'Un menu, s'il vous plaît,'* and you know how to swear in Spanish, so you're thinking, why do I need any more, *pendejo*? I can just translate it on my phone anyway, why do I need to learn *c'est dingue, non? . . . No es importante . . . Tidak apa-apa . . .?*

And I say, *'Oui, c'est vrai. Però . . .'*

Apart from the sense of self-respect you might get from conversing in another tongue, you will earn the respect of locals for bothering to at least attempt to speak their language. Not only that, there is a growing body of evidence that suggests learning another language has unexpected benefits. Language can improve your short-term memory. A Swedish research team asked some volunteers to take part in a study of a group of students who were taking ten-month university courses. By the end, volunteers who were taking the language course had nearly a 30 per cent better retention rate of people's names. Their research also suggested that language study affects four key areas of the brain directly related to memory.

Learning a language can help you in your decision-making, too. Studies from the University of Chicago suggest that people with language skills are better equipped to pick up nuance and subtlety in a situation. Perhaps because these are the very things which we tend to miss when speaking another language, so maybe this is what prompts us to work a little harder in that department. And this in turn leads to

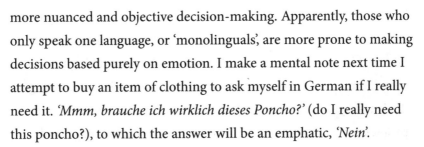

more nuanced and objective decision-making. Apparently, those who only speak one language, or 'monolinguals', are more prone to making decisions based purely on emotion. I make a mental note next time I attempt to buy an item of clothing to ask myself in German if I really need it. *'Mmm, brauche ich wirklich dieses Poncho?'* (do I really need this poncho?), to which the answer will be an emphatic, *'Nein'*.

Learning a language can help you to stay focussed, it helps you practise a thing called 'inhibitory control' which is what filters out background noise and helps us concentrate. It activates the brain, which in turn improves our ability to multitask. *'Je takez le rubbish out, et à la même temps je watchez le Netflix.'*

It increases our perceptual sensitivity. Come on, you know you've always wanted that. This is the ability to notice things, particularly tiny

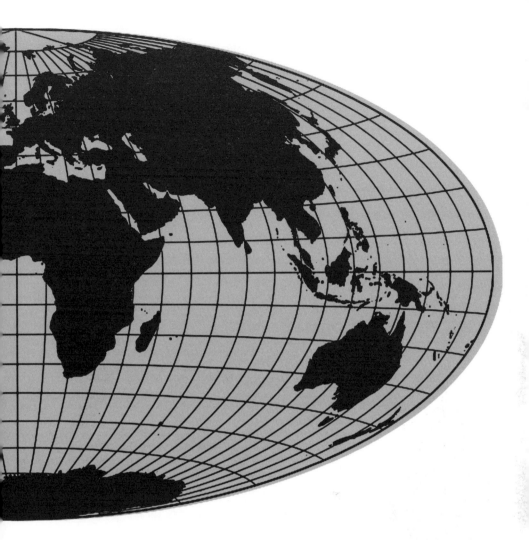

changes in facial expression or vocal modulation. I'm sure dogs have this, but in humans it's more about a finely tuned awareness of your surroundings.

It can give you better cognitive abilities. Startling research from the University of Edinburgh suggests that learning a language can prevent brain ageing, even in adulthood. Reading, verbal fluency and intelligence were improved in a study that ranged in age from eleven to people in their seventies. The strongest signs were for reading and general intelligence. Learning a language can prevent cognitive decline. It can protect against Alzheimer's and dementia. That's got to be worth a shot.

And here's another great benefit: it helps you to improve your own language. By focussing on grammar and construction, you end up with a net benefit to your mother tongue. Learning another language makes you a better writer, speaker and communicator.

All this sounds marvellous, but the most extraordinary claim comes from the University of Lund in Sweden. Lund is in Skåne, a county in the south of Sweden famous for its open, rolling countryside and the backdrop to the *Wallander* series of books by Henning Mankell. OK, it probably features more in the television adaptations which would often show a police car speeding along traffic-free roads through acres of well-tended farmland, a golden light shimmering off the bonnet, which could be mistaken for a Saab advert.

One of Lund's most celebrated alumni is Carl Linnaeus, who I am sure you know is the founder of zoological nomenclature, the naming of all living things in his favoured language, Latin. When you refer to yourself as *Homo sapiens*, you can thank Carl Linnaeus for that. So, it's fitting, I think, that Lund has identified a huge advantage in being multilingual. Their study showed that learning another language can increase the size of your brain.

I know, right? Are you for real, Swedish brain size promise-mongers?

I am an enthusiastic speaker of as many languages as I can, albeit with wildly differing results.

I attempted to order some dumplings once from a Beijing street seller. Dumpling in Mandarin is, I am sure you know, *'jiaozi'*. And the pronunciation requires you to start high on 'jee', go low on 'ow', then back up again for 'zi' which itself is pronounced 'tser' with a flat intonation. 'Jee-ow-tser'. I practised this in the hotel room, and thought I had a passable accuracy.

When I asked the seller for 'jiaozi', I was met with blank incomprehension bordering on fear. He looked as if I was asking him for his licence, or if he had any money. When it became clear what I was after, he smiled and laughed. 'Oh, Jee-ow-tser!' which sounded identical to what I thought I'd said.

Indonesian is a language which over the years our family has become familiar with. And we use it every day at home, mainly because it simplifies so much of the daily ritual. 'Bahasa Indonesia', literally 'Indonesian Language', was created to be a common language for all of Indonesia after it achieved independence from the Dutch. A country of seventeen thousand islands and hundreds of languages needed some unifying tongue. Its basic form is so user friendly. It's not inflected, you don't need participles, a verb can be a suggestion, an action, an exhortation. 'Belum' can mean 'not yet', or 'not quite', or 'your reversing car has about another four inches of space before it hits the lamp post.' *Sudah* can mean 'already', or 'I've had enough' or 'your car has hit the lamp post.'

Every night, before we eat, I say an Indonesian word that is so much simpler than English: 'makan'. In Bahasa Indonesia, the everyday language is quite simple and straightforward. Verbs are not parsed, one word can mean 'food', and 'Do you want to eat?' 'Have you eaten?' 'Let's eat!' I love the sound of it. Yes, of course we have our own exhortations: 'Dinner is served!' or 'It's on the table!' or maybe just 'Let's eat!' But there's something joyful and earthy about the consonant-rich, two-syllable clarity of 'Makan!'

SIMPLICITY

35

I am standing at the prow of a large log raft, floating gently down a river in rural Sweden. I feel a bond with this craft, an ownership, as I have spent many hours with my family and a gang of friends assembling the logs and lashing them together with rope. The water is a deep green, cool and clear, full of silver bream and pike. I wield a huge wooden pole in gloved hands to fend the raft off from the slow approaching outcrop of rocks. It's a job I have assigned myself, and after a few days of this, I've become quite the expert.

OK, it's only prodding a huge pole into the riverbank now and again, but it's essential for our smooth progress down the river. The current is slow but powerful, so if the raft drifts near an obstruction, sandbank, rocks or overhanging trees, I let the pole slip through my hands into the deep water, find the riverbed, push down, then swiftly pull it up and as the raft responds we glide past the rocks. I lean on my pole and grin at my newly acquired skill, like some recently qualified gondolier.

I take a satsuma break from poling duties and perch primly on a slightly-too-small camping stool. In the distance, a couple of moose cross a shallow section of river far downstream. I start to reach for the camera, but something stops me, and I just watch instead. Their comically ungainly antlers bob about, making them look like two men delivering a coat rack. A momentary flare of the sun's reflection on the water causes me to squint and turn my head, and when I look back, the moose are gone, leaving our little group alone again, drifting through acres of pine forest as if we are the only folk left – rafters in an unspoilt paradise – and in this moment I have a revelation.

Now, before I get to that, you may have detected a distinct Nordic bias to this whole book, to which I say, yep, fair enough, but you just can't write about happiness without a sprinkling of Scandinavian influence, it's not possible. The Nordic countries consistently occupy the top ten of the 'World Happiness Report', so they must be doing something right. Or maybe it's because my ancestors are from these parts that I am drawn here by some ancient pull of my Neanderthal DNA, like a bearded salmon returning to my Palaeolithic spawning grounds. My DNA test also revealed that I am 60 per cent Danish, so there's every chance my ancestors would have been Vikings. I'd like to think they were not so much the violent, pillage-y kind of Vikings and more like Viking admin, or longship maintenance.

I've dived with whales off the Barrier Reef, with sharks and turtles in the warm seas of the Eastern Moluccas, swum with giant manta ray, free-fallen hurtling through the air, paintballed like a demon, paddleboarded around World Heritage sites, climbed active volcanoes at dawn, been fêted by kings, queens, princes and at least one sultan that I know about. I've held a Gibson Flying V aloft and roared like a man possessed in front of sixty thousand metal fans during the Sonisphere Festival at Knebworth House in a biblical storm of epic dampness.

But on that day on the River Klarälven, as I drifted silently aboard this wooden craft, propelled by a shimmering current, ripples of diamond sunlight dancing across my sunglasses, it was a moment equal to any of my more pulse-quickening experiences. Is it just ageing that has brought this on? The feeling that, as we get older, we naturally want to slow down and appreciate the simpler things? Maybe, but on this occasion, I don't think it's the case. I look around at our rafting ensemble and the ages of this merry band range wildly. A mix of kids and adults prepare food, or dangle fishing lines from the back of the raft, or just bask in the sun. We talk about anything and everything or lapse into a meditative silence. Others laugh and amble along the riverbank, gathering wild raspberries. It's so ludicrously idyllic that it could be a scene from that charming tale of rural Swedish life that Thomas Hardy never got around to writing, *The Raspberry Gatherers*.

The whole caboose brings together so many of my tickets for happiness that it hardly seems real. Simplicity, clarity, nature, friendship, physical challenges are all here, with bells on.

In the late afternoon, someone paddles ahead on a paddleboard, and finds a suitable mooring for the night. Sweden has a wonderful law, a right to roam or 'allemansrätten', which allows you to camp anywhere you like, within reason. It's legalised wild camping basically, which unless someone ruins it for everyone else by camping on a roundabout, or a crazy golf course, is enshrined in law for perpetuity. In Britain wild camping is largely illegal, it's only the Scots who are deemed responsible enough to camp unsupervised.

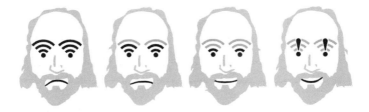

We set up camp and light a fire in a clearing near a small beach, where the raft is tethered to a birch tree. Some kind of magic begins to work on me on a camping trip. It's a sensory experience that begins with sound. As soon as I hear the soft click of tent poles being assembled, I can feel a smile beginning to appear on my face which broadens as I heft the mallet and hammer pegs into the ground.

It's the act of stepping back from the general whirl of life that appeals to me so much. As the guy ropes are tightened around the pegs and the camping stove is lit, I can feel a weight lift from my shoulders, and in some forgotten fold of my cerebral cortex, a tiny remnant of hunter-gatherer DNA twitches into life.

Overnighting in the outdoors leaves you feeling happier, more optimistic and energised.

With friends and family, it's a great team effort, a bonding experience, a shared purpose that, dare I say, might bring you closer emotionally with your fellow campers.

You'll most likely be closer to nature too: you will sleep when it's dark, you will hear birdsong and you will rise with the sun.

I can honestly say that there has not been one camping experience that hasn't put a smile on my face in some way. Even the mudfest-lose-your-car-keys-knock-over-the-dinner ones. Camping encourages you to be resourceful, self-reliant, and most importantly, it creates experiences, which are the solid investments that provide a good return of happy.

Ah, but what about the lack of showers and hot water, Bill, eh? And the toilets? And the bugs? The lack of Wi-Fi? Well, that's all part of it. In fact, some of my fondest memories of camping were when it was at its most basic. I recall a wonderful week under a tarpaulin in the Sumatran jungle with my wife and son when he was tiny. It was about as far away from a trouser press and minibar as you could get, but amidst the bugs and leeches this was an unforgettable delight, and unexpectedly relaxing.

My wife and I both love travel and the outdoors, and have done since childhood, so when our son was born, we were quite taken aback that so many parents gave us dire warnings about how all this would have to end. 'You want to go travelling? Forget it. Camping? Oof! That's not going to be easy with a little one, no, no, it's B & Bs in Dorset for you from now on.'

We took this as a direct challenge to our wandering ways, a camping gauntlet thrown down. A quick-dry, EzyPack RipStop travel gauntlet if you will. No more roughing-it-style trips off the beaten track for us, you say? OK, we'll see about that.

Fast-forward to our young family wedged into a narrow log canoe with an outboard motor, skimming up a river in central Sumatra, watching giant turtle lumber off the riverbank and slip into the water, while orangutan crash gracefully about in the canopy overhead.

As I said, the campsite was a tarpaulin on the riverbank, strung between two trees. The anxious voices of other parents rang accusingly in my head: 'What about mosquitoes? Bites? Germs? What's the hygiene rating?' We were of course vigilant with regards to the insect repellent and cleanliness, and the boy was well cared for, and we kept a watchful eye as he played endlessly by the river with the dozens of village kids who were intrigued by us and came to hang out with us every day. But we quickly realised that our son was in such good hands that we could relax enough to grab the occasional nap. And every night he slept soundly in his buggy, with a mozzie net strung over his cradle, asleep in seconds, lulled by a chorus of crickets in the jungle night.

So here I am again camping by a river, only this time a Swedish pine forest is the backdrop. It's perhaps not as exotic as the Sumatran jungle, but no less agreeable.

I sit in the dark under the moonrise, cradling my wine, watching the embers of the fire glow, and I realise, this is all it takes for peak living. Oh, and my satsuma-fuelled revelation was straightforward. It occurred to me that if I could experience this feeling once in a while, I would be replenishing a deep well of contentment. It's a decent amount of happy in the bank, for when the boiler breaks down on a cold February night, when things go wrong, when we lose someone.

The night air was chillier now the fire had gone out, so I crawled into my tent and fell into a deep, dreamless sleep. I woke up at sunrise to the sound of birdsong. And as I emerged into the dawn I was greeted with a perfect blue sky and the ticklish curl of wet grass under my bare feet, and momentarily all seemed right with the world.

LOVE

36

In a study by Pennsylvania and Stanford Universities, twelve million blogs were analysed for words associated with happiness. Younger bloggers used words like 'excited' and 'elated', while the older writers were 'relaxed', 'peaceful', 'calm'.

What older people are doing writing blogs when they could be hugging trees and paddleboarding is beyond me, but here is more evidence, if any were needed, that our perceptions of happiness change over time.

I think of love in a similar way, as running parallel to this change in our view of happiness. The two lines occasionally cross, and maybe then diverge, but they're never far apart. And like happiness, love manifests itself in different ways that represent the stages of our lives. There's our love of our parents, our pets, our friends, then romantic love, companionship, love of nature because if you're lucky enough, it'll be a boon companion for the whole bumpy hay-ride, hitched to your wagon regardless of road quality.

I realise my good fortune to have met someone like my wife. We now are more than thirty years together, through all manner of adventures, and despite the usual ups and downs, we've been lucky with the weather. 'Generally fine, with some chance of cloud, and occasional drizzle, followed by sunny spells.' Happy Ever After conjures up a romance where there are no arguments and no tragedy, where you just sit gazing at each other over a raspberry flan until the End of Days.

I think about our marriage, and our long relationship, and I realised many years ago that we were in uncharted territory. Neither of us has been together with someone for this long. So rather than the usual caveats you hear about people becoming bored with each other, I see the opposite. Every new day is another step into the unknown, a new adventure.

We met many years ago when we both had big hair. It was the eighties, so this was acceptable. There were no mobiles; we had not yet joined the internet. It seems almost impossible to imagine: how on earth did we communicate? How did we get things done, book holidays or go on washing machine forums? We met while I was living in London, and she was in Edinburgh, and we communicated via regular letters, as I told you in my essay on letter writing. We lived together on a houseboat for a year, and believe me, this is a serious test of any relationship, one that, if you pass, will forge an even stronger bond between you. After a few months on the boat, she rightly commented on the squalor, which I, as a single man who had been living alone, had perhaps consciously overlooked. 'What's wrong with it?' I asked indignantly. 'It's damp,' she said. 'It's not that damp,' I countered, uncertainly. At that moment she pointed to a large mushroom growing out of one of the doors that I had hitherto chosen to ignore. The mushroom was a turning point, a fungal pivot on which turned our future together, towards some new, drier accommodation, preferably on land.

Love in all its forms can be a perennial supplier of happiness. Love persists through the tough times, and endures through all weathers. It is a single note that sustains, like the sound of a bowed double bass resonating deep below all the other show-offy sounds.

But I do not believe that love is a passive state of mind, a settled condition of drowsy, low risk contentment. For happiness to work you need to lace it with a bit of spice, a bit of mischief. This characterises our marriage. There's often a lot of banter, some sarcasm, and a general healthy spark to our daily discourse. As I said in my show *Limboland,* contentment is knowing that you're right.

Happiness is knowing that someone else is wrong.

ABOUT BILL BAILEY

Bill Bailey is a comedian, musician, actor, author, and documentary maker. He lives in London with his wife and son, and a small menagerie of animals.

He is the author of *Bill Bailey's Remarkable Guide to British Birds*.

THANK YOU

I'd like to offer my thanks to all those without whose help, skill and patience this would not have been possible. Thanks to Luke, Susan, Kelly-Anne, Will and Seán for all their support. Thanks to Lee Stone and Victoria Gaisford at Lee and Thompson.

Special thanks to my brilliant editor Katy Follain, for all her encouragement and perceptive suggestions, and all the excellent folk at Quercus.

Also special thanks to Joe Magee, for his unique insights and inspired visuals, along with Fiona, Floyd and Sylvie for their invaluable help and feedback.

My heartfelt thanks to all those who have featured along the way, whose company and friendship have contributed so much to making the memories on which this book relies.

There are so many to mention here, but for their long-time friendship I single out my old pals Sean Lock and Nick Blackbeard, with whom I've shared so many adventures, and my father Christopher, whose encouraging words spurred me on to begin this book in the first place.

And my son, Dax, who has been there for all the trekking, camping mountain biking, paintballing, skydiving and now inspires me to do more.

And my wife, Kris, whose unwavering support, perceptive comments and constant encouragement helped to keep the whole project on track.

The End

All drawings by Bill Bailey

All graphic and photo-illustrations by Joe Magee